# The Calm Lake
## Satchidananda

Errol Ishwara Cowan

# DEDICATION

Lillian

This book is dedicated to my mother, Lillian Echt Cowan. She gifted me with my life, intellect and creativity. Lillian left this earth all too soon and before I could express my heartfelt gratitude to her. She supported the evolution that enabled me to write this narrative.

Calm Lake

# CONTENTS

| Chapter | Title | Page |
|---|---|---|

## ACKNOWLEDGMENTS

- *HH Sri Swami Satchidananda inspired the author to write this book.*
- *Very valuable review and editorial suggestions were the result of the numerous hours devoted to this project by Natasha Paige Farmer.*
- *Photos in this book were provided by Swami Dhivyananda Ma, Jeeva Abbate, Satchidananda Ashram, the author, Natasha Paige Farmer, yogaville.org & swamisatchidananda.org*
- *Barbara Turner located and scanned several very important photos for this book most of which she took during an India tour while travelling with the author who was her husband at the time. The photos that Dr. Turner provided are identified with* ☀.
- *The photo of Swami Satchidananda in Switzerland is by Rudraksha108 / Maithreyi Andre Marcela Andre - Own work (Original text: "I created this work entirely by myself."). Licensed under Creative Commons Attribution-Share Alike 3.0 via Wikimedia Commons http://commons.wikimedia.org/wiki/File:SatchidanandaSwitzerland.jpg#mediaviewer/File:SatchidanandaSwitzerlandg is noted with ***
- *The photo of Swami Satchidananda opening Woodstock is by Mark Goff - my own collection. Licensed under Public domain via Wikimedia Commons - http://commons.wikimedia.org/wiki/File:Swami_opening.jpg #mediaviewer/File:Swami_opening.jpg It is noted with ****
- *The cover photo for this book was provided by Satchidananda Ashram-Yogaville.*
- *Dan Grogan provided a candid photo of the author sans spectacles.*
- *The noted artist, Stephen Madhavan Holland provided his artwork of Swami Satchidananda and an inspirational story about how the swami helped him to regain his wellness.*
- *Leela Marcum provided a poignant vignette for the book.*

# INTRODUCTION

This book was written to fulfill the request of HH Sri Swami Satchidananda and is published in honor of 100 years that have passed since his birth.

In the late sixties the swami became widely recognized by the media as a spiritual icon and an influential advocate for interfaith dialogue. I knew him to be an extraordinarily wise person. Thousands of people knew him and hundreds of thousands benefitted from his teachings.

This book began as a small collection of brief vignettes that seemed to write themselves about my experiences with the swami, his teachings and his organization. For more than thirty years of my adult life, I was very fortunate to spend hours, days and sometimes weeks assisting and working with the swami, who eventually became my mentor. He inspired me to continue growing beyond what is typically considered adulthood and discover tranquility in a joyous realm that I never knew existed.

The evolution of my relationship with my mentor and his teachings occurred during an interesting epoch in American history. When I told my stories to my friends who knew him, they remarked that the tales were unique and interesting enough to merit a wide audience. I took their advice and decided to include some concepts and practices of yoga in my book for those who are unfamiliar with my teacher.

By organizing, distilling and articulating what I learned over the years, writing this book helped me to heal, reinvigorate, and better understand my mentor's teachings. I am grateful that he told me to write about my experiences as this was a good reason to take the opportunity to integrate all I had learned. Perhaps he also felt that this book might add something to the next chapter of your life story.

My interaction with the wisdom and the everyday human attributes of a great yoga master is covered in these writings. It includes explanations of what he taught and some examples of the results. No one person can present an adequate catalogue of all of the wisdom that my teacher embodied. This overview is myopic because it is limited to my understanding, opinions and interpretations.

The limitation of my account is illuminated by my teacher's tale of 3 blind men encountering an elephant. When one is asked to describe the pachyderm and touches its trunk, his report might be of a serpentine creature. The second man who touches only a leg would have a different description while the last man of the trio who touches the tusk would disagree with both of his comrades. Likewise, my stories offer subjective perspectives on selected facets of the teachings of Swami Satchidananda.

The swami's Integral Yoga® is one of many viable pathways from adulthood to true maturity and beyond, into a realm of tranquility and happiness. If we decide to take it, the journey is not far. The destination is here inside and we will realize that we have already arrived.

-Ish Cowan   *December 22, 2014*

HH Sri Swami Satchidananda

# 1 ∞ THE END IS THE BEGINNING ∞

Stairway to the Story

Wispy clouds decorated the deep blue sky as otter cavorted in the cove and the last guided kayak trip of the day returned. My bucolic world would soon be shattered and I would be unexpectedly racing across the country from my home and retreat center called Doe Bay Village on beautiful Orcas Island.

My retreat center was at capacity with a yoga group accommodated in the rustic cabins, as well as hostellers, campers and day-users of the spa and café. I was sitting in the office when my partner, Priya breathlessly entered and said that I had a call from my brother Eliot, the shaman. Picking up the receiver I exclaimed "Well, hello fellow, it's so nice to hear from you for a change! How was Mexico?" I opened my mouth to crack a joke but before I could Eliot blurted out, "Ish, I called to tell you how sorry I am." "Sorry about what, Yogeshwar?" I asked. He exclaimed, "Oh, I guess you have

not heard that your teacher passed away!" I did not know. I quickly
ended the call and dialed Yogaville in Virginia. My heart sank when I
learned that it was true. My mentor's lifeless mortal form had already
been transported back to Virginia. The final ceremony and
entombment was to be held the very next day.

There was no time to feel sorrow and there was not a second to
lose. Priya packed for both of us in 20 minutes and we raced the 30
miles across the island in my barely functional AMC Pacer. We
arrived at the ferry landing right after the gates of the mainland
ferryboat were closed. We were tense because of the need to catch
the only 'red-eye" flight to the east coast.

The ferry attendants must have sensed our desperation. They
reversed the ferry and opened the gates for us. One and a half hours
later we disembarked on the mainland dock. Then we drove for two
hours without stopping and arrived at Seatac airport fifty-five
minutes before the redeye flight to DC. After lavishing a king's
ransom on the airline for last-minute tickets, we were the last to
board.

Morning dawned over National Airport as our plane arrived. I
rented a car and we drove non-stop for three and a half hours. Then
we arrived at Satchidananda Ashram-Yogaville, VA which was a
community we had helped to create and our former home. Upon
arrival, jumping out of the car before Priya could park it. I ran up a
monumentally long and high stairway that accessed the building
where the ceremony and entombment of my teacher's remains were
being held. I seemed to levitate as I jumped over three and four steps

at a time. This was quite a feat for my corpulent, non-athletic frame in the oppressive 105 degree heat.

When I arrived on the top landing, hundreds of people dressed in white were silently standing around the closed door to my teacher's final resting place. When Priya joined me I reached for the handle as it was being locked. An old friend who was inside with others who were participating in the last minutes of the final ceremony unlocked the door and quipped, "Well, the prodigal son slides-in at the last minute just like he always did at our meetings. Why am I not surprised?"

There was an open casket near the entrance decorated with flowers. We approached it and were the last arrivals to bid a loving farewell to my teacher, best friend, surrogate father, inspiration, taskmaster and confidant for more than 30 years. With the exception of five other people who were present that day, I had spent more personal time with my teacher than anyone else during the thirty year period. Because I was breathless and exhausted from the 20 hour cross-country sprint and arriving just in time to see my teacher laid to rest I did not feel much in the way of emotion.

Seven years after that day I returned to Yogaville and climbed the same long unforgettable stairway. I wept at the marble casket for 30 minutes. During that time, the sorrow that I felt transformed into magnificent peaceful bliss. While I was crying on the outside I still felt his presence and on the inside my heart was joyous. As I left my teacher's final resting place, I remembered that I had experienced the same kind of intense blissful feeling fourteen years earlier.

It was in the darkness of a late autumn evening in 1995 while I was driving my mentor through the farmland country between Richmond and Buckingham on State Route 60, close to Cumberland, Virginia. Returning to Yogaville from his public talk in Richmond we were reminiscing and laughing heartily about some of our experiences during the 1970s. There was an extraordinarily mirthful feeling to this exchange that seemed to transport me into a dimension where I experienced myself as the perpetual essence of disembodied, unbounded joy. Suddenly remembering that I was driving, I willed myself back to "reality" instead of continuing to drift inward, upward and outward towards infinity. Mirthful moments then melted into minutes of silence. Then my passenger softly said, "Write a book about your times with me."

# 2 ∞ BEAT & HIP ∞

San Francisco in the late 1950s was electric, eclectic and eccentric. National media attention was focused on the *San Francisco Renaissance,* populated by the "beat" generation that was centered in North Beach. Its authors, poets and musicians were the movers of the movement at that moment. Ferlinghetti, Rexroth and Ginsberg set a tone critical of American wars, suburban sterility and senility. This attitude was expressed in their poetry, prose, and Zen life-style. On weekends I put on my black turtle-neck sweater and beret to conform to the *beat generation* dress code and joined many others forced to stand outside of the packed *Coexistence Bagel Shop* and listened to beat poetry read by its authors who were backed by live jazz music.

When Ginsberg's little book, *Howl* was published in San Francisco by Ferlinghetti, its reception and the publicity conferred widespread fame on Alan. He became the movement's iconic figure. It was Ginsberg and Gary Snyder who were the role models that led to the counter-cultural norm of drug-taking, meditation and practices of Buddhism in this sub-culture. This led to a mushrooming interest in Eastern philosophy, meditation and yoga.

The beat culture in San Francisco eventually faded but some elements were transplanted when the movement morphed into the counter-culture and lifestyle of the "hippies".

The term *hippie* was derived from the 1940s, starting as *hepcat* (a person called a *cat* who is *hip*), later changing into *hipster* in jazz influenced beat parlance and finally to *hippie* as a description of the emerging younger generation that took the torch passed on by the receding beat movement.

The epicenter of countercultural currency shifted a few miles to the west from North Beach to the corner of Haight and Ashbury Streets on the periphery of Golden Gate Park. Ginsberg and some of his beat generation comrades made the transition and appeared at hippie events. They became accepted as leaders and were primary early influences on the burgeoning movement. Likewise, I also made the transition from counterfeit beatnik to ersatz hippie.

The *Human Be-In* was held in Golden Gate Park on January 14, 1967 and it was a prelude to San Francisco's Summer of Love, which drew international attention to the Haight-Ashbury as the epicenter and symbol of the new American counterculture. I attended the historic *Be-in* along with 29,999 other long haired young people. This event was influential as a model for the movement. There was no admission fee and the program lasted all day and through the night. Free food was provided by benefactors called the "Diggers" and free dope was also available for those who wanted it. Music was provided by Jefferson Airplane and the Grateful Dead to name a few of the many groups who contributed their efforts. Ginsberg appeared on-stage and led the chanting of *Om*, an important sound that is part of some yoga meditation practices.

Toward the end of the 1960s, Alan Ginsberg and other notables from the faded beat generation continued to promote concepts, culture, religion, philosophy and yoga from the Far East. These elements leached into and were absorbed by the emerging youthful counter-culture. During this time, the Beatles who were the most influential musicians and trend-setters in the world went to India and took-up meditation.

Experiences during the psychedelic era motivated some but not all of the new generation to recognize the value of yoga. As psychedelics began to take their toll, interest evolved in ways to access higher consciousness without the hazards of drugs. This trend was a magnet for domestic and foreign teachers of Eastern religions and yoga. They came to instruct unprecedented numbers of enthusiastic young Americans.

Fascinated with hippie life-style and culture I became a *day-tripper* and except for my 9 to 5 job, I was to be found frequenting the Haight-Ashbury district. During that time my future teacher whom I had not yet met was developing a rapport with the counter-cultural movement in its embryonic stage on the East Coast when he was flown-in by helicopter to preside over the opening of the historic Woodstock Music Festival.

Swami Satchidananda Opening Woodstock ***

# 3 ∞ GIFT OF THE BUSH FAIRY ∞

One day while meandering in the park next to the Haight-Ashbury, I happened upon a group of pony-tailed young men in orange vestments who were playing drums and finger cymbals. They were situated on a mound near a grove of tall eucalyptus trees and chanting a repetitious phrase that was written on a huge sign:

"Hare Krishna, Hare Krishna, Krishna, Krishna Hare, Hare"
The chant was pleasant and almost hypnotic. Even though I did not know its meaning I joined the chanting. Months later, I read about Sri Krishna. He was a good looking cowherd who lived in India in ancient times. He had blue skin and played the flute. Krishna was said to be a wise sage and a divine incarnation who had many female followers called *gopis*

After chanting ended, the leader of the pony-tails suggested that I join them at Golden Gate Park the following week for a Krishna chanting procession to the ocean followed by a feast. I agreed to go for the free meal.

The next week at the park procession I was positioned in front of a massive ornate chariot decorated with flowers. It had a ten foot high platform with a throne-like chair. The back of the cart was ten feet taller than the platform. A stern-looking dark-skinned old Indian man was seated on the throne. He wore robes and a gargantuan garland of gardenias. His name was A.C. Bhaktivdanta Swami He was the leader from India who revived the ancient tradition of chanting to evoke Sri Krishna, whose role as a deity was central to the sacred Hindu scripture, the *Bhagavad Gita.*

When the chanting procession had travelled about half-way through the park, a fair haired female fairy-like hippie magically materialized from behind a bush and approached me. I thought, "Hmmm, I must be better looking than I thought for this goddess-girl to approach only me, particularly when there is a famous man with an impressive throne-cart behind me." Her eyes were twinkling but alas, it was not because she was charmed by my imagined good looks. She said nothing as she handed me a small poster and then immediately disappeared back into the bushes. I wondered, "Maybe she is one of Krishna's gopis?" I never saw her again but her simple gift changed my life. It was a poster imprinted with a photo of a bearded, dark-skinned foreign-looking man. The deep look in his eyes made me think, "This person knows something that I want to know." The poster exhibited a long Indian name and it announced a yoga lecture at the Unitarian Church on a Saturday night in July of 1969.

Gift of the Bush Fairy

After attending the Krishna procession I drove a few miles past the Golden Gate in Marin County to my cottage in a redwood tree-filled canyon of Larkspur. I tacked my poster given to me by the bush fairy on the wall so that I could see it from my bed. I would gaze at it and wonder what profound wisdom was behind those eyes. I also tried to figure out how to pronounce the strange looking name that was printed on the poster.

# 4 ∞ TRUTH KNOWLEDGE & BLISS ∞

Swami Satchidananda

One day I started to wonder what the name on my wall poster meant and decided to do some research. The name was *Swami Satchidananda*. I discovered that there were several different English translations of the name. Merriam-Webster Dictionary defined *swami* as "a Hindu ascetic or religious teacher: a senior member of a religious order - used as a title". The Merriam-Webster Encyclopedia of Religions added "A swami is an ascetic or yogi who has been initiated into a religious monastic order." The *Oxford English Dictionary* gave the etymology as "Hindi *svāmī* master, lord, and prince, used by Hindus as a term of respectful address." Wikipedia recently noted that

"*Svami*, is used as a prefix followed by a given monastic name. The term usually refers to men, but can also apply to women who have taken the oath of renunciation and abandoned their social and or worldly status to follow this path. The monastic name is usually a single word without a first and last name."

According to my present understanding, English language authorities gave a somewhat limited meaning to the noun *swami*. I now know that the term refers to a person who wants to become selfless and serve a higher cause or monastic lineage. These individuals typically renounce attachment to possessions, personal gain, sexual relations, family ties and egoism. They can be dedicated to a religion or some other purpose without the expectation of direct personal benefit. Some live reclusive monastic lives, while others function as Hindu priests or teachers. Some swamis practice and teach yoga. Swami-hood is often adopted by people who believe that it is a more certain pathway to attain the goals of a religion or of yoga practice.

The last name of the person on my poster was *Satchidananda*. I learned that it is a combination of three Sanskrit terms: *sat*, *chid* and *ananda*.

Wikipedia offers the following about these three words:

**Sat** "Truth, Absolute Being - a palpable force of virtue and truth" Sat describes an essence that is pure and timeless, that never changes.
*Cit*): "consciousness, true consciousness, to be consciousness of, to understand to comprehend".
*Ananda* (noun): "bliss", "true bliss",", happiness", joy", "delight", "pleasure"
**Sat-Chit-Ananda** or **Saccidānanda** is the Sanskrit compound form of the 3 words, which can be translated in various ways: "Eternal Bliss Consciousness" "Absolute Bliss Consciousness" or "Consisting of existence and thought and joy"

Once, when asked, the swami translated his name to mean "existence, knowledge and bliss. At first, the name *Satchidananda* was difficult for me to remember and to pronounce. It was conferred upon my mentor at the time of taking monastic vows from his renowned yoga master, *Swami Sivananda* at his Himalayan *ashram* (spiritual retreat community) beside the Ganges River in India. The name literally describes the goal or culmination of yoga practice.

Swami Sivananda & Swami Satchidananda at Sivananda Ashram

Seeing my poster photo changed my impression of what a swami looked like from reading comic books as a youngster. Back then I saw cartoons of a turban-wearing duck sitting cross-legged on a mountain with a crystal ball.

The swami's name sounded foreign, exotic and imposing to me, but not to one young lad. When the swami and I were travelling on a ferryboat from Victoria Canada, a youngster came up to him and said, "Hello! I know who you are." The response was, "Oh, who am I?" The reply was, "You are Salami Sawancha!" The swami roared with genuine laughter.

# 5 ∞ CALM LAKE ∞

Symbol of the Inner Clear Calm Lake - Lotus Lake at Yogaville, Virginia

Finally the day for the yoga talk announced on my wall poster arrived. I went to the Unitarian church where it was being held and got there early but so many people were already seated that I had to take the very last available place. Introductions were given by radio personality Les Crane. To my pleasant surprise he was joined by Tina Louise, an attractive TV star on whom I had a big crush. Her photo was on my wall long before I put up the swami's poster right next to it.

As the speaker was introduced, I saw that he was a tall, slender, dark-skinned man in his late 50s with a long beard and long black hair that contrasted with his orange floor-length robe. The swami sat cross-legged on a throne-like chair. After making a few remarks, what the speaker said really grabbed my attention:

## THE MIND SHOULD BE LIKE A CLEAR CALM LAKE

The calm lake image of the swami appealed to me because I had spent my childhood summers at a cabin in Bass Lake, Indiana. I never was able to catch a fish and the water was so shallow that adults could wade across it. Despite these drawbacks looking at the lake always calmed my mind. Being there was a peaceful hiatus from distressing family circumstances and disruptive events at my family's central city apartment in Chicago during each school year.

The swami talked about the benefits of having a calm mind. In closing, he suggested that the audience sample his idea of a clear calm lake. To this end, he led a chant. It sounded more peaceful than anything that I had ever heard. The audience alternated responsively with his chant:

### OM SHANTI OM SHANTI OM SHANTI OMMMMM

After a few minutes the chanting trailed-off into still silence. In its enveloping peace, I felt elevated beyond body and mind. The experience was very different but also very familiar. I realized that this man's eyes in my poster had been inviting me to inhabit this peaceful new dimension. I went to the talk as an agnostic but I later expressed my feelings to a friend about the chanting with the period of silence that followed. I explained, "Being there made me feel like there might be a heaven and a God". I wanted to be able to return to the speaker's calm lake and needed to know how to do this on my own at anytime.

After his talk ended, the speaker introduced Vijay and Shree Hassin from New York City who had recently rented an apartment on Balboa Street in San Francisco. They lived and were about to teach yoga classes there under the name of the *Integral Yoga Institute (IYI)*. The next day I went to their Balboa Street apartment and attended their very first class.

# 6 ∞ THE FIRST STEP ∞

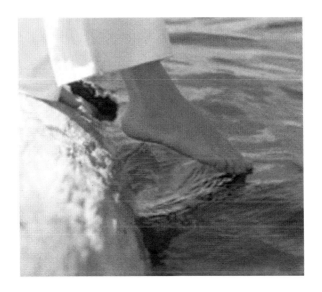

I started to take yoga classes out of a desire to revisit the "calm lake" experience that was introduced by the swami during his talk. He claimed that his IYI classes supported such an experience. Yoga practice seemed an even better idea when I learned that the swami was 57 years old at the time and the perfect picture of health due to his years of yoga practices. At his age, he was flexible enough to model advanced pretzel-like postures for photos in his book, *Integral Yoga Hatha*. Years later he told me that even though he had not practiced yoga postures since the age of 45, his body and mind became trained well enough to become permanently relaxed without continuing to do yoga postures. Later in his seventies, he could still assume complicated yoga poses.

As I began to take classes and absorb the swami's writings I found that what he taught was basically common sense. Some of it was like what is found in modern psychology and some religions - but he labeled it yoga. I learned that the swami's teachings were almost the same as the original version that emerged in India centuries before the advent of modern Hinduism, Judeo-Christian religions and Islam. Later on, the Western world became familiar with yoga as a result of the conquest and inclusion of India in the British Empire.

Some people think that yoga is a religion. This is an understandable mistake because some of its practices are similar to religious rituals. Even so, yoga is simply a collection of methods for mind and body conditioning to promote health and self-evolution. As a matter of fact, in the final stages of yogic practice there is a naturally occurring transcendence of yoga and religious concepts and deities. Evidence that yoga is not considered a religion is to be found in the English language. The names of religions are capitalized while the noun, *yoga* is not.

The question of whether or not yoga is a religion was tested in a California court during 2013 in Encinitas, CA. The city school district offered yoga classes as part of the curriculum to be taught to grade school children. The plaintiffs were groups of fundamentalist Christians who argued that yoga is Hinduism and teaching it in public school violated separation of "church and state". The court ruled in favor of allowing yoga in the school district. The case is an example of the misunderstanding that many Americans have about yoga in thinking that it is Hinduism. In fact, yoga writings have been documented by historians to be centuries older than the emergence of Hinduism.

Perhaps some people think that yoga is a religion because many yoga teachers include Hindu Sanskrit chants, cuisine, deities, mythology, language and clothing along with the basic elements of yoga. Indian cultural trappings can be helpful but are not necessary. This addition makes yoga more interesting to most people but repugnant to some. When an Indian cultural dimension is added to yoga it is akin to tasty curry powder added to an already nourishing plate of vegetables. With or without Indian customs, yoga is a collection of techniques that facilitate wellness, peace of mind and personal transformational experiences.

Swami Satchidananda said that even though yoga is not a religion it can play a supportive role in religious practice. He also emphasized that the teachings of all religions along with those of yoga are compatible. To this end, symbols of the major world religions are represented in the Integral Yoga® logo that the swami designed.

Integral Yoga Institute Logo (Yantra)

The yoga system can be practiced by itself or in combination with any religion. For example, some groups now offer *Christian Yoga*. This can be likened to name brand medicine while yoga by itself can be considered the generic version. Either "medicine" will benefit the user.

Yoga is sometimes defined as its goal or end state which is the union of body, mind, environment and spiritual aspects of a person. Along with the various degrees of such a union there is increasing awareness of the inner Self.

Although yoga is older than Judeo-Christian religions, some of its practices are similar. Religious prayer has equivalency in yoga practice as devotional attitudes and ceremonies known as the path of *bhakti yoga* along with meditation which is called r*aja* or *japa yoga*.

Charity and community service is taught as a virtue in most religions. It is also recommended by modern mental health professionals. For a Christian, charity is a duty, for Jew it is a law and in yoga it is a practice known as *karma yoga*. A nuance that the Swami gave to the karma yoga practice of serving others was the explanation that it is not helpful to the charitable person unless his or her deeds are performed without expecting anything in return – not a religious conversion of the recipient or even a "thank you". Religions and yoga diverge where religious traditions declare prayer, devotion and selfless service must be performed only in the name of one specific god, prophet or creed. Irrespective of religious labels, almost all rituals and devotional practices are viewed by yogis as valid beneficial tools for the refinement and enlightenment of the individual.

The room where I took my first yoga class was decorated with flowers, yoga symbols and pictures of famous yoga masters. Classes were filled with young enthusiastic long-haired men and women that looked like hippies. In the manner true to the counter-cultural philosophy of that era, there was no set price for the classes and any amount of money, fruits or anything else was considered payment. One prospective student even tried to offer some marijuana in exchange for a class.

As I explored the classes offered by the Integral Yoga Institute, I learned that it not only encompasses a collection of *hatha yoga* physical postures but also includes *raja yoga, karma yoga* and an assortment of other practices. I discovered that there was an accumulation of benefits ranging from physical well-being to emotional balance, extraordinary abilities and progress toward life-changing perceptions and epiphanies.

Yoga practice is said to culminate in self-discovery, the characteristics of which correspond with what the humanistic psychologist Abraham Maslow termed *self-actualization.* Interest in Maslow's work waxes and wanes as psychology moves through different phases and schools of thought. Even so, his work has enduring relevance to yoga. To my knowledge, Maslow's writings do not directly refer to yoga but his markers of *self-actualized* people as listed below accurately describe Swami Satchidananda and other yoga adepts.

- *Acceptance and Realism* about themselves, others and the world around them.

- *Interest in helping others* and identifying solutions to problems in the extended community. This is motivated by a sense of personal responsibility and ethics.

- *Spontaneous thinking and behavior.* Even though there is conformity with rules and expectations, there is also an openness and ability to think and act "outside the box".

- *Maintenance of personal independence and privacy.* This is not to the exclusion of others all of the time, however ample time is allocated to seclusion.

- *Consistent appreciation of life and the world with wonder and awe.* Even simple daily experiences become a source of inspiration and pleasure.

- *Experience of moments of intense joy, wonder, awe and ecstasy* that Maslow termed *peak experiences.* After they occur, people feel inspired, strengthened, renewed or transformed.

Even though the term *self-actualized* can describe people who have greatly benefitted from yoga there is a paradoxical feed-back loop between yoga practice and outcomes. This is because the characteristics of self-actualization are also what yoga writings prescribe as part of yoga practice. Maslow's markers such as the will to help others and partial seclusion have been a part of yoga practice for centuries.

The term *yoga* is commonly taken to mean its system of practices but the peak experience it catalyzes, sometimes called *samadhi* is a more accurate definition of yoga. From my own experience and observation, I summarize the relationship between yoga practice and its culmination in a peak experience this way:

*Yoga practice has the ability to relax, purify and calm the body and mind. These conditions are supportive of intense concentration leading to meditation which can facilitate the practitioner's realization that he or she is different from body and mind. Concurrently, there is a dawning awareness of his or her self as peaceful, joyous, imperishable and un-changing. This experience is a realization called "samadhi" or "yoga" which is the ultimate goal of the practice of yoga techniques. Because of the heavenly and timeless feeling in such a state, some people who enter the state describe it as leaving the body, going to heaven, experiencing communion, divinity or God.*

It seemed to me that my "calm lake" experience facilitated by the swami's first lecture was a very small taste of what samadhi might be like. When I learned that yoga was a pathway that can access it, I decided to enter the water and be a committed student.

# 7 ∞ TEMPORARY OUTAGE ∞

Swami Satchidanda Meditating in his Himalayan Cave *

There is a spectrum or hierarchy of peak experiences and states of being that yoga literature refers to as *samadhi*. The experiences are categorized according to the quality, intensity and duration of the experience. The most robust samadhi precipitates an individual's disassociation from body and mind and the permanent awareness of the difference, along with perpetual joy. Less intense experiences of bliss and joy in samadhi are revelatory and inspirational but temporary.

Samadhi does not occur only because of yoga practices. This inner state is recognized and experienced in other paths to personal growth and religions. It is also called satori, state of grace, enlightenment, self-realization and divine communion. In addition to yoga practice, devotional rituals, profound introspective epiphanies as well as some intense emotional or physical experiences have been known to catalyze a samadhi. Conscious and un-resisted natural death is another peak experience that yogis consider a type of samadhi.

I was perplexed when I first read about samadhi and even more so about *Mahasamadhi* which means the great or mega-samadhi. It is an individual's final and complete disassociation with body and mind at time of death. It is said to be the highest and best experience of unlimited bliss. At first I thought that the whole idea of living was to stay in a healthy body as long as possible. Death sounded like a "bummer" to me and I wondered how leaving the body temporarily or permanently could be the joyous occasion that it was touted to be.

Two years into my yoga practice, one of my meditation experiences provided the answer when I seemed to exit my body as my mind became very calm. For me this was an indescribably joyous event. The experience was so intense that afterward, my subconscious unlocked, releasing a repressed memory of my near-death experience that occurred when I was 15 years old.

I was a teen when my father took me to see a powerboat race on a beautiful lake ringed by weeping willow trees. It was the noisiest and most exciting event that I had ever seen. Apparently, back then I did not appreciate calm lakes and preferred agitated water. After seeing the race, I wanted to be a racing boat driver. As an attempt to coax better teen-age behavior out of me, my father and grandmother promised to give me a racing boat if I was good for a whole year. The promise had the desired effect. The horns fell-off my head and were replaced by angel wings and a halo! Responding to my miraculous metamorphosis the family threw a surprise birthday party for me and presented me with a huge birthday cake and a small racing powerboat.

One sunny day during a racing practice session I wore a life jacket as usual but carelessly left my racing helmet behind. I became distracted for a moment as I was zooming along the shoreline of the Red River and crashed into a much larger cabin cruiser. As my head hit the bow of the cruiser, my vessel splintered into pieces. After this happened I did not lose the sensation of forward motion. Speed and engine noise were replaced by a feeling of silent slow motion as I gently floated forward, and up into the sky. Unaware of having a body, I had the sensation of expanding for miles around and upward. I also had a feeling of peace, happiness and unfettered freedom.

During my out-of-body experience, my mortal frame was drowning unconscious and face-down in the water. The expanding joy bubble that I became suddenly burst and I was sucked back into my body. The people in the cabin cruiser had resuscitated me. I did not remember this event until two decades later when this scary childhood experience surfaced while I was meditating. This recall emerged because my near-death boating experience was about the same as my experience in deep meditation. In both situations I was beyond body and mind and the experience was wonderful. Reflecting upon these two significant events persuaded me that samadhi and mahasamadhi were genuine inner states and they were to be welcomed.

My earliest spontaneous experience with meditation and a near-samadhi occurred even earlier when I was six years old. Although I have very few childhood memories, this one I can clearly remember until this day. I was supposed to be taking my afternoon nap but instead I stood up on my bed and stared at myself in a big mirror on the wall. For a while I did not recognize the reflected image and I wondered "Who is this and how did he get here?" After staring at the reflection some more, I felt elevated, weightless and very peaceful. The answer to my questions came in silence. I experienced myself not as a child but as a timeless vast entity that had the will to be present in this world.

My childhood bedroom epiphany and boating accident experiences were to be surpassed by those triggered during my adult life through exposure to my teacher and his teachings. They were all accompanied by an intense blissful feeling that at the time seemed to be unending. On second thought, it probably is unending. When my mind was tense or distracted with selfish concerns, the joy remained in the background, waiting until my mind was less busy to re-emerge. Nowadays, when I remember to remember my peace or simply stop obsessing about anything and everything, a feeling similar to having the best, most uninhibited inner giggle-fest in the entire universe once again returns.

Now that my body and mind have become somewhat disciplined through yoga, its practices are still beneficial but they are not always necessary to relax into my higher self. Merely holding my breath or remembering the feeling of a moment of mirth when my laughter erupts is adequate to restore awareness of inner peace and joy.

My mentor wrote that very few people take-up yoga to seek its ultimate benefit which is the life changing state of a robust samadhi. He said that of those rare people who are interested in seeking the highest states of yoga, only a very small percentage will ultimately stick with it and be diligent enough about the practices for long enough to reach their intended goal.

Although yoga offers lofty possibilities, most Americans practice yoga in pursuit of limited helpful outcomes such as body toning, flexibility, wellness and stress reduction. Irrespective of a student's motivations, yoga and its lifestyle can improve self-discipline, balance in diet, breathing and peace of mind. I personally would prefer to take an extra step and experience being out of my mind in samadhi.

# 8 ∞ BODY OF KNOWLEDGE ∞

Hatha Yoga at San Francisco Integral Yoga Institute

The current popularity of specialized yoga courses is a testament to its ability to make life healthier and more enjoyable. My teacher established a facility known as *Satchidananda Ashram–Yogaville* in Virginia. In addition to continuing Integral Yoga® instruction, it offers applied yoga programs focused on benefits of interest to the general public. These courses help to generate income to maintain the yoga community. Specialized courses currently offered at the time of this writing include such topics as *yoga for the female pelvic floor, yoga for the special child, life coaching, and yoga beach vacation, senior's restorative retreat* and *a healthy lifestyle yoga retreat.*

The classes that I took when I started yoga classes consisted of rudimentary instruction and practice in hatha, yogic breath control and chanting. While some yoga schools emphasize one yoga technique, classes designed by Swami Satchidananda taught a combination of techniques which is why he called it *Integral Yoga®*. It includes physical and mental relaxation routines, meditation, breathing regulation, devotional practices, discipline of the mind and non-identification with thoughts and desires. A student's capabilities, taste and temperament can determine the specific mix of these yoga techniques that he or she practices.

Most people think that yoga consists only of physical postures called *asanas* which are practiced systematically in routines that are called *hatha yoga*. This aspect of yoga improves flexibility, eliminates toxins in the muscles, deepens breathing, improves glandular functions and relaxes the body and mind. Asanas are often paired with breath control exercises called *pranayama*. When paired together these two practices can energize, purify and relax both body and mind.

At first, physical postures were not comfortable for me due to my corpulent, toxin laden body. After one month of regular practice, the asanas began to pay dividends as I became very relaxed by the end of each session. During an ending-up period of *deep relaxation* it felt like I was being transported to the swami's calm lake. I had the sensation of floating and being enveloped in a peaceful cloud.

As I continued with my hatha yoga practice, I experienced increasing levels of peace and relaxation. I no longer lost energy when my biorhythms nose-dived at 3 PM daily. As a result I also had spare energy and was able to work efficiently long into the night.

Although I regularly practiced hatha yoga for years, my body never became as flexible as most newcomers. My first hatha instructor remarked that my short, stocky body of Eastern-European heritage presented limitations on the ability to assume advanced poses and he was correct. Later on, when I became a hatha yoga instructor, my beginning students were typically more graceful and limber than I was. This did not matter because hatha yoga is not a competitive sport. It confers its benefits irrespective of the limitations of various body types. My inability to master advanced pretzel-like asanas as an instructor did not prevent my students from progressing and enjoying their benefits.

Fifteen years after beginning yoga practice I became a principal in a consulting firm in a new office building in upscale La Jolla, CA. where I had a huge executive office. In one corner there was an easy chair and a side table with a framed photo of my yoga teacher and I meditated there during lunch hours. When I was away on a 3 week business trip, one of our secretaries would sneak into my room and rest in my easy chair during her free time. She recounted that without knowing about mediation she lapsed into that state while sitting in my little corner. Our secretary also reported having dreams about the man in my framed picture and eventually became one of the swami's followers.

One day an associate came into my office and said. "I have a health problem and my doctor says it's from stress. He told me to find a way to relax. In our office environment this is difficult. I would like your help because you seem to be the most relaxed person in our office. I want to learn your secret." For two weeks I taught him hatha yoga postures and yogic breathing in my office after work hours. After that he reported that his symptoms subsided and his doctor told him to continue with the relaxation. My associate related his experience to others in my office and before long I was teaching yoga postures after work to 5 more co-workers.

# 9 ∞ SOUND THINKING ∞

Sanskrit OM

Meditation is a familiar aspect of yoga for most people. It consists of practice concentrating all mental activity upon one thing such as the breath, a repetitive sound sequence called a *mantra*, a thought or an image. IYI mantras are repetitious Sanskrit phrases that are melodic and chanted internally. They usually include the syllable *Om*. Mediation is the primary ingredient of the branch of yoga that Swami Satchidananda called *japa* which is considered part of *raja* yoga.

Any mantra that feels elevating and comfortable or one suggested by a teacher can be used by a yoga student. Other types of meditation can employ a prayer, a popular song, a name, or any phrase such *as Amen, Adonai, Allah; I am at peace, Hallelujah, Hail Mary* or anything else that can be easily repeated to facilitate concentration and peace of mind. Different mantras can have varying effects on the mind, ranging from tranquilizing and relaxing to energizing.

Beginning meditation is practice in not allowing the mind to wander to other thoughts while repeating a mantra. As a concentration aid, some people use rosaries and move one bead every time the mantra is repeated.

For me, meditation was easier said than done. At first I did not enjoy sitting on the floor attempting meditation in class with crossed legs for long periods because they became cramped. My mind resisted meditation by acting bored and thinking about everything except the mantra which was the intended object of concentration. Never-the-less I kept going to classes but I sat on a chair when I practiced at home.

*The mind's tendency is to run here and there, from one point to another. To focus the mind during meditation, try this: When you realize that your attention is away from your meditation object, gently bring the mind back to its focal point. Whenever it wanders away, bring it back. When you bring a running mind back again and again, that is called concentration. No one actually meditates in the beginning. The mind keeps on running away. Bring it back. If you keep on doing that, one day you will have the success of keeping it focused for at least five minutes. When that happens, you will be meditating.*
*-Swami Satchidananda*

Various branches of yoga are simple in theory but in practice resistance from an undisciplined mind can make mastery of its techniques and achievement of its goals very difficult. With everyday practice, the ability of hatha yoga and meditation to strengthen my body and discipline my mind gradually increased over a several year period. I started to notice that after a combined hatha and meditation session, my mind stayed slowed-down for most of the day, allowing me to calmly observe and keep an emotional distance from troublesome thoughts. This increased my ability to think more clearly and objectively.

As I advanced in meditation, all the thoughts in my mind started to disappear during a session. At first this scared me but later on I experienced a blissful interlude of eternal nothingness. In the void, there was the absence of anxiety, desire, strife and pain. In their place was only peaceful, effervescent joy.

In addition to feel-good aspects of hatha yoga and meditation, I experienced positive impacts on my job performance because I was more relaxed each day, irrespective of the ambient stress in my office. The ability of my mind to concentrate expanded exponentially with daily meditation practice thereby increasing my ability to analyze information and issues at my work. With greater access to my intuitive powers provided by yoga practice, problem-solving and decisions came easier. As a result I became much more efficient in my work.

In undergrad college I made barely-passing and some failing grades. After I had been doing yoga and meditation for some time, I returned to study in graduate school with great ease and my grades were outstanding because of my increased ability to concentrate. After I graduated with a PhD degree and became a professor, I was able to work on research faster than my colleagues because of my newly acquired powers of concentration.

Calm Lake

# 10 ∞ ELEVATOR ∞

Nerve Purifying Breath. Art by Stephen Holland

Yoga breathing techniques are called *pranayama*. There were two that Swami Satchidananda said should be practiced daily as good preparation for meditation. The first technique consists of alternating rounds of diaphragmatic breathing called the bellows breath. This increases energy, alertness and clears the lungs and mind. The second technique is a nerve purifying breath. It consists of rounds of inhalation through one nostril while closing off the other, then exhalation through the other while the first nostril is closed off. The breathing should be slow and deep. I found this to be very relaxing.

Conscious, regulated breathing has health benefits as I discovered before I became serious about regular pranayama practice. During a checkup my MD said that I had high blood pressure. Although I was reluctant to pester my teacher with personal issues, I panicked and called him for advice. His response was "People make too much out of this. Just breathe more." As a result I made it a point to make sure I did yogic breathing every day and it did lower my blood pressure.

Most pranayama techniques include breath retention which can increase tranquility in the mind. During some breath retention episodes I lost the sensations of thought and anxiety. By conditioning myself with meditation, yogic breathing and hatha yoga, I had unknowingly trained myself to trigger sublime states through breath retention alone.

In addition to health benefits, regulated breathing can facilitate enhanced abilities of the mind and senses. One of my friends who constantly practiced yogic breathing developed an ability to accurately see the future for other people. Another friend could levitate his body and move small objects through the air. I often found myself with ability to read the minds of other people as a result of my disciplined breathing.

My mentor explained that the breath regulates many bodily functions including energy flows in the body. The life force energy in the body is called *prana*. That is why yogic breathing routines are called *pranayama*. Yoga practice not only endowed me with mastery of breath so that I could control my blood pressure, stress levels and my thought process. My peak experiences and epiphanies occurred during deep, slow breathing that transitioned into extended retention of my breath.

At the time of this writing I have the ability to quickly un-stress or spontaneously enter into meditation simply by consciously regulating my breath to be slow and deep and offering my exhalation into the inhalation for about two minutes.

My positive experiences with yogic breathing as instructed by Swami Satchidananda led me to investigate *The Science of Breath* and *The Science of Psychic Healing* by Yogi Ramacharaka (William Atkinson). These books highlighted advanced techniques and advocated the use of pranayama to promote wellness and healing. Some of this information contributed to improving my health and enabled me to help others reduce their physical and emotional afflictions.

# 11 ∞ FOOD FOR THOUGHT ∞

As a part of a yogic lifestyle Swami Satchidananda recommended abstinence from smoking, mind altering substances, as well as alcohol and meat consumption. He maintained that organic vegetables, fruits and vegetarian diets are supportive of healthy bodies and calm clear minds. The swami advised against meat consumption, noting that when animals are slaughtered they get fearful and secrete hormones into their bodies that when eaten adversely affect humans. I respected my teacher's opinions but I was not willing to curtail the use of something just because I was told to do so.

I continually used substances known to be toxic even after I started yoga. Never-the-less, my system detoxified because of the practices. One day while I was meditating I perceived that nicotine in my blood stream from smoking was affecting my clarity of thinking on the job and my ability to concentrate in meditation. I immediately and *effortlessly* stopped smoking and never had the desire to start again. Two months later, I went through the same process with alcohol consumption.

About the same time that I was parting company with smoke and beverage, I began divorcing from flesh-food consumption. This process started earlier in life and ended later than my other intake modifications. As a young Jewish lad, I was conditioned to be careful about meats because of the religious laws about keeping *kosher*. This tendency was magnified when my mother who was on a modest budget fed me inexpensive pot roasts from a pressure cooker. This kind of meal had capillaries which squirted blood when I cut into the portion on my plate. After many such incidents, I only wanted meat with a look and texture of something other than what it was, such as ground round steak. Then there was a mafia-related horse meat scandal in the city where I was living. During that year my mother avoided taking me to dine out and refused to buy "beef" to serve at home.

By the time that I started yoga and listened to the swami's talks about health hazards of consuming meat, I had already been eating all of the veggies on my plate while avoiding most of the meat. The fact that my new yoga friends were eating tasty vegetarian dishes influenced me not to ingest traditional flesh slabs on my plate ever again.

About one year after starting yoga and becoming a vegetarian, I tried once again to take-up carnivore-ism. I was planning a trip to Europe and wanted to sample *la cuisine Francaise* which included meat entrees. A fortnight prior to departure to the old country I went to a deli and purchased a large pastrami sandwich in order to prepare myself for a continental meat-eating binge. After consuming half the sandwich, I was very ill for two weeks until leaving for Europe and I never ate meat again.

Eating in Europe included fish entrees as a result of my new self-imposed dietary restrictions. I ate so much sea life that I overdosed and became perpetually disgusted at the idea of consuming my finned friends. Now left with fewer dietary choices, I ordered two eggs sunny-side up on the morning after returning to the new world. They glared at me from the plate and addressed me in English. They rudely and emphatically insisted, "Don't eat us!" I responded affirmatively to the resentful twin embryos and have since honored their demand by not ingesting any of their successors.

## 12 ∞ MEETING MY MENTOR ∞

Swami Satchidananda & Ishwara Cowan. India, 1977 *

Within the first year that IYI classes started at the Balboa apartment a few of us looked for a larger, more permanent home for classes and events. The first day that we went looking for a place I whined, "But our institute has less than $100 in the bank account!" We eventually found a suitable place and money magically materialized from numerous sources including my own check book. We accumulated a down payment but as a group we did not have the ability to qualify for a mortgage to complete the purchase. We searched high and low for a loan without any luck. Eventually the seller came to know and appreciate our group so much that she decided to finance the balance of the purchase price herself.

Turreted multi-story wood Victorian buildings in San Francisco were favored by hippies such as us. We found a great one, unlike any other. It was built of stone and had the requisite turret. It was four stories high and had survived the 1906 San Francisco earthquake. It was in original condition. Our hatha instructors and a few students moved into the new yoga group home.

IYI San Francisco

Even after the IYI house had been acquired, I preferred to live in Marin County tucked away in my little cottage surrounded by redwood trees. Six months after I started to take yoga classes Swami Satchidananda was returning to our area for a visit and I was asked to volunteer my cottage-in-the-woods for his stay. I gladly did so. The home was very small so my girlfriend and I moved out for the week to make room for the swami and his secretary. Just before we vacated, it dawned on us that perhaps we should wash our pile of dirty dishes and put long overdue clean sheets on the beds. I could not take my *Pooh-dog* with me so I figured the swami and his secretary would just have to feed Pooh and put up with her.

After the swami arrived on the following day I returned to my cottage and tried to sneak onto the porch to retrieve my mail but I spotted my guest in the yard with a dustpan and broom. To my embarrassment he was cleaning-up Pooh-dog's dog-pooh! There is a saying that when the student is ready, the teacher appears, but I never imagined it would have been under such circumstances!

Looking back at the time that the swami was staying at my cottage I now realize that what happened there was symbolic. On the day we met the swami and I chatted on the porch and exchanged greetings. He said, "I shall have many homes with you." That statement proved to be prophetic. For the first 14 years of our association, I was his host many times in Larkspur, Fairfax and Santa Barbara. During that time, I also helped to create his yoga institutes and communities in San Francisco, Santa Barbara and San Diego.

When I first met the swami in-person, he was busily cleaning up my yard. This suggested to me that he was a humble person and liked order in his life. Cleaning my yard was also symbolic of things to come. Over the following years he gently encouraged and inspired me to clean-up and simplify my life.

When Swami Satchidananda saw evidence of my lifestyle during his stay at my cottage, he must have known that he had a big task ahead of him. In public talks he routinely advised against taking mind-altering substances, eating meat, drinking alcohol and smoking. At that time, my house contained a Turkish water pipe, rum soaked wine dipped cigars and handmade cigarettes of questionable content. An abundant selection of meats occupied the freezer with an ample stock of beer and wine that populated the refrigerator. He diplomatically never said a word about any of this to me.

The swami's stay at my cottage cleaned up another mess in my life which was the uncertain relationship with my girlfriend. His stay precipitated our temporary move away from each other and the intended temporary separation became permanent. She went to

Greece. I relocated and settled in Berkeley. That marked the end of the relationship.

In the days and years to come I was to learn much about the guest who was in my home. Swami Satchidananda looked like a tall, well-groomed, older hippie. Some thought that he looked like images of Jesus of Nazareth. He made a favorable impression on the counter-cultural generation, speaking about themes dear to their hearts: peace, love and joy. He enjoyed a high profile in the U.S. because one of his sponsors was the internationally celebrated counter-cultural artist Peter Max who had invited the swami to come to the USA from Sri Lanka.

Swami Satchidananda. Artwork: Peter Max

After arriving in New York City, the swami gave informal talks to Max's young hippie friends. They became a permanent group of admirers that formed around him. They insisted that he stay in the

US instead of returning to his ashram in Sri Lanka and provided the financial means for this to happen.

The swami was playful, loved to make puns and always had a great sense of humor. He had fun renaming places and things. He called enchiladas "Cincinnatis". Santa Barbara's Carrillo Street he referred to as "Gorilla Street". When he spied a young woman stacking rocks at Yogaville, he quipped, "Are you getting stoned?" He had a gentle but charismatic personality and he was always well-versed about current news and technologies. There were interviews and articles about him in the New York Times and the Wall Street Journal. The swami became an iconic media figure after flying-in by helicopter to open the historic Woodstock rock festival with his *Om Shanti* chant.

Swami Satchidananda Opening Woodstock

# 13 ∞ SERVE GIVE FLEX ∞

Swami Satchidananda with Temple Elephant in India 1977 *

My body type would not allow me to become a hatha yoga superstar, but there was hope for me as a yogi. According to what the swami taught, I had been practicing other kinds of yoga without even knowing it. Any of the branches of yoga are supportive of its ultimate goal which is peace and joy. *Karma yoga*, known as the yoga of dedicated action is one such branch. The swami was an excellent model for this in addition to the other practices. He sacrificed self-interest and his own comfort in favor of serving anyone who asked for his help. I resonated with his example because assisting other people or their groups came naturally to me throughout my life.

Karma yoga practitioners can typically be found working on something. The karma yogi practices training the mind to do every action dedicated to benefit something or somebody and to avoid being motivated by self-serving agendas. Even eating, caring for one's body, making money, and looking attractive can be performed with the attitude that these things are for the purpose of serving others in the best possible way. A bus driver can practice karma yoga by developing an attitude that his or her main purpose is to help people get from one place to another. A secondary concern for karma yogi bus drivers might be their work earns money to sustain them so that they can continue to provide service to the travelling public.

During my first two years of learning from the swami I joined with others in his institute who were also spending increasing amounts of time as karma yoga volunteers. I served as my teacher's bodyguard, secondary social secretary, itinerary planner, travel companion, financial contributor, errand boy, chauffeur, business and financial consultant, and corporate executive for the growing number of West Coast yoga institutes.

At the swami's request I frequently performed the service of co-hosting and entertaining his visitors. He met with authors, media reporters, academics, spiritual leaders, politicians, movie and music personalities as well as his yoga students. Some visitors had a mild apprehensiveness about a meeting with him. This might have been similar to my childhood reaction when I went to visit a kindly department store Santa Claus at Christmastime.

Although the swami's personality was friendly and polite, his appearance was a radical departure from that of most Americans. He was an internationally known celebrity and authority on an esoteric subject derived from an exotic culture. He was also considered to be a spiritual giant and holy man. With such reputation and aura when some people met individually with him it is understandable that they might have felt slightly intimidated.

Perhaps I was given the role of co-host because of my relatively conservative appearance, my university faculty status and the fact that I circulated in both a yoga environment and the workaday world unlike my mentor's other helpers. At times, my presence acted as a buffer and served as a lightning-rod that helped some guests feel more at ease during their visits with the swami.

My teacher would occasionally have me assume the role of scapegoat when I was helping him entertain visitors. To make a point to his guests he would criticize me instead of them for what they were doing. I understood that this was his way of teaching his guests without bruising their egos too much. Being criticized for something that I did not do also tested my ego.

I handled all my karma yoga work in addition to my divergent roles of tenured professorship, litigation support roles, court witness assignments, yoga teaching and property brokerage responsibilities. Hatha and meditation gave me abundant levels of energy to do it all. Karma yoga practice taught me to have appropriate attitudes in playing all of my roles successfully.

In performing my work for the swami, I tried to remember to adopt the karma yoga attitude of selfless service. My purpose was to train myself not to expect acknowledgment, money or even a "thank you" for anything I might do. My mentor constantly provoked me to check if my service to him was without self-serving motivations. In private he was usually friendly with me. In public settings it was sometimes a different story. He could be reproachful, impatient, unreasonable, disagreeable, formal, casual, silent, affectionate or indifferent.

Whenever I developed a tinge of self-importance about my roles in working closely and spending a great deal of time with the swami, he would immediately do something to humble me. A good example of this was during a meeting when I was sitting close by his side. He stared at me blankly and addressing the assembled group he said, "Some of you may be thinking that this guy must be spiritual because he is with the swami so often. He is not spiritual. I am just using him."

In order to assist the swami I not only had to be humble but I also had to be flexible because of his constantly changing roles of holy man, host, celebrity, public speaker, mentor, adviser or friend. Each role change modified the way I had to interact serving my teacher in order to be of assistance. The shifting roles and changing treatment from my mentor were good life lessons about the need to always to be flexible. They were also helpful to reduce my ego which often obstructed my willingness to be flexible.

I wasn't the only one that learned lessons about flexibility by experiencing a greatly varying relationship with the swami. Some were able to bend because they intuitively tolerated and acted according to the constant flux in his roles. Others misunderstood the teacher's loving intentions to refine them. A few found the constant changes to be too much to endure because they expected a teacher to be "perfect", consistent and unchanging.

My mentor never talked to me about the need for flexible role playing. Even so, I felt an unspoken agreement that we were on the same team with both of us adapting to whatever roles might be of best service to others. As a result of the constantly changing interaction with my mentor, I learned to persist in performing tasks and maintaining a positive attitude no matter what changes occurred. Importantly, I began to carry this self-discipline into other aspects of my life, work and relationships.

The outside world reinforced what I was learning from my mentor, when I dined with a couple married for 45 years. I asked for their secret of a successful long-term relationship. My hostess echoed what I learned from Swamiji when she replied "Honey, from my side of the story I've got to be my man's sister, mother, lover, business partner, daughter and friend."

Flexing with the changing needs of the swami taught me how to cope with different personalities and roles in life in order to get along with and best serve others.

*To combat stress, which is the main reason for problems of the mind, do away with expectations - don't even expect a thank-you note. If you make no appointments, you will never have dis-appointments.*

*The secret of life is simple. Play your part well but don't identify with that part. How? Remember who you are. You have roles to play in life. Act well but, at the same time, do not forget that you are acting. Then you are safe.*
*–Swami Satchidananda*

*Adapt, adjust, accommodate and realize!*
*-Swami Sivananda*

# 14 ∞ DHARMA & KARMA ∞

Swami Satchidananda with Students and Monks in India *

To be in one's *dharma* is the best way to live life. It is also called "right livelihood" and means working at something that is not harmful to others. It comes naturally because it is compatible with a person's talents and interests. Various people have different dharmas.

People become miserable when they work at what they think they *should be* doing instead of what they really *want* to do. Such mistakes are made when people prioritize desires for prestige, fame, money or to meet cultural or familial expectations. As mentioned earlier, karma yoga is the path of self refinement by replacing selfishness with the attitude of helping others.

For me, my dharma and karma yoga service is optimal when I combine them. I have always been naturally drawn to creating, maintaining, improving as well as developing groups and communities. I also enjoy researching and teaching. These things became my life's work. At some point I realized the combination of my ability, interest and work in these fields was my dharma. My primary motivation was not fame and fortune but to help others. So, this was both my dharma and my karma yoga.

At the age of 14, I formed a boys club at the local "Y". At 15, I started teaching weekly jazz appreciation classes there. Intuitively I was starting to fashion my life around dharma and karma yoga principles. All during my high school years I hosted social get-togethers for my friends at my home every Friday evening. I formed a men's fraternity chapter in college and became its first president. In graduate school I studied housing, community development, real estate and town planning. Later on, I became a professor in these fields. After that I served as a consultant to cities, counties and Fannie Mae. Finally, I consulted with community builders and then I became a developer.

Gurudev easily found ways for me to combine my community focused dharma with my practice of karma yoga. As a result, I helped to incorporate the Integral Yoga Institute of California and establish three of its California locations. I also served as the first president of the Yogaville Council at its national headquarters in Virginia and for a while was director of the Integral Health Clinic there.

My karma yoga experience in the establishment of yoga institutes and communities inspired me to create my own commercial adaptations of the yoga community model.

In 1981 Swami Satchidananda, his secretary and I visited Orcas Island in Puget Sound in connection with a seminar that he gave. We were taken with the island's beauty and serenity. This influenced me to launch Doe *Bay Village and Retreat Center* on the island. My operating model included yoga classes, vegetarian cuisine, an emphasis on self-growth and service to the public.

Doe Bay Village and Retreat Founded by the Author

I later established a second location with similar programs known as *Hidden Valley Ranch Retreat Center* in Santa Barbara.

Unlike my teacher's facilities, my retreat centers were established as profit making entities but service to the public and staff was the priority in my management decision-making. Preservation of and honoring Mother Nature was also a guiding principle. While I operated my retreat centers I continued to serve the swami's institutes and communities and at the same time served as a university professor of community and environmental planning.

My primary interest at the retreat centers was the principle of service instead of feeding my bank account. I could have become extraordinarily wealthy by placing my investments in other ways but I chose to use my funds to perform my dharma as karma yoga. Looking back at that part of my public service gives me a feeling of self-approval, satisfaction and joy.

In performing administrative tasks for my teacher's institutes as well as my own retreat centers I found that working with and directing employees or community members was the most difficult part of my chosen work. I found it hard to motivate even well intentioned people to function well together for common good instead of pursuing their individual personal agendas. Selfishness, egotism and immature attitudes were a constant disruption and a trigger of frustration for me.

Reflecting upon my administrative difficulties I marveled at my teacher's ability to cope with larger issues, greater numbers of people and scattered facilities as head of his organization with hundreds of staff serving thousands.

I complained to the swami when I became aggravated with the behavior of some of his followers He replied with compassion, "Just remember Ish, they are all children." The people in question were not minors chronologically speaking but I understood what he was saying. Just as children can be uncooperative or self-centered at times, many adults who have not completed their emotional growth can act irresponsibly. I realized that the swami's perspective empowered his ability to understand, tolerate, love and guide those who followed him.

My teacher's simple advice about understanding adults as oversized children changed my life. It infused me with a sense of tolerance and understanding of people that I would have previously perceived as troublesome. This allowed me to be a happier, more compassionate person and an understanding manager.

Three weeks had gone-by after my mentor made his "They are all children" comment and I woke up laughing in the middle of the night. I had realized that meant I was also a child! From that time on, I started to love and accept myself like a parent loves a child. This released me from self-recrimination for my shortcomings, increasing my self-esteem and appreciation of my truly positive qualities.

# 15 ∞ LOVE & DEVOTION ∞

Rev. Ishwara Cowan in a Puja Offering *

*Bhakti* is one branch of yoga that was taught by the swami. This form is the easiest to practice and understand for many people because of its similarity to Judeo-Christian devotional rituals. Bhakti comes naturally to emotive people. Gods, goddesses, saints, teachers, gurus, idols or other inspirational icons can be used as objects of love and worship. Devotional and loving feelings are expressed in symbolic rituals called *pujas*, or prayers, chanting, singing, dancing, art, or written words. Scriptural study can also be part of the practice. At first I did not favor practicing bhakti because it seemed to be the same kind of rituals as found in typical religious practices in Judeo-Christian churches and synagogues. Even so, I could not deny that bhakti activities lifted my spirits and put my mind at ease, elevating it into meditation.

Some fledgling yogis find that bhakti is a comfortable

continuation and intensification of their previous religious practices and beliefs. From the yogic perspective, intense devotion has the ability to quiet the mind as it focuses on its object of affection to exclusion of all else. The mind turns away from disruptive thoughts in favor of realizing the capacity of the heart to love. Culmination of bhakti practice occurs when the loving devotee experiences unification or merging with the object of his or her devotion. This is accompanied by a feeling of fulfillment with no remaining desires or anxiety.

As a former musician I took note (pun intended) of the way that my mentor used bhakti in the form of Sanskrit devotional chants to set the mood and moderate the energy of audiences at his public talks. If an audience seemed lethargic and unable to pay attention, he would address this by leading a responsive, rhythmic upbeat chant. As the audience participated, the room became energized and the people were better able to focus on what the speaker had to say. On the other hand, if an audience was unable to settle down, the swami would lead a soothing slow, meditative chant and the energy in the hall would become calmer.

Observing the effectiveness of using devotional chants to improve audience attention I began to reflect upon the power of music to influence behaviors. This prompted me to see if I could use chanting and singing to modify my occasional gloomy and hyper states of mind.

I began to use Sanskrit chants, melodic prayers in Hebrew and popular songs in English for my own mood modification. The *Om*

*Shanti* chant of my teacher proved to be a very effective tranquilizer for me. I also employed tunes from Disney such *as Zippity Doo Dah.* A Johnny Mercer song from the 40s was very effective in elevating my mood. It started off: *You've got to accentuate the positive, eliminate the negative, and latch on to the affirmative: don't mess with Mister In-Between.*

One useful Sanskrit chant that I learned was ancient. It evoked the elephant-headed, human-bodied Hindu deity, Ganesh. I found the *Jai Ganesha* chant to have a powerful mood elevating quality.

Representations of Hindu deities such as Ganesh are rendered in vivid colors. To my eye they have a cartoonish quality. Imagining this rotund comical character dancing around always improved my mood. When I was asked for help by others who were depressed, I suggested chanting and imagining Ganesh dancing. This never failed to induce a smile. Because of this effect I came to appreciate the merits of Bhakti yoga.

Dancing Ganesh

# 16 ∞ ADOPTING A MENTOR ∞

Teacher & Student *

Before I met my yoga teacher I tried reading several self-improvement books and religious scriptures but found them boring, difficult to understand and hard to apply. Trying to adopt their methods seemed inefficient, fraught with pitfalls and dead-ends. They were too easily misinterpreted because they were based upon oral traditions that reported utterances of deceased teachers or prophets. Most scriptures were written in ancient foreign languages hundreds of years after a great teacher lived. They were often colored by the perception or agenda of the scriveners.

Compounding the problem of interpreting and understanding

ancient written wisdom was the fact that cultural changes over time often diluted, obscured or froze the teachings into dogma once they were written down and dispersed across the globe over hundreds or thousands of years.

By the time that I encountered Swami Satchidananda I had given-up on scriptures and self-help books. He revived my interest in self-improvement by introducing me to yoga. When I experienced its effects and learned more about it I considered it as a potentially good path to my self-growth. Many practices that he taught were intended to discipline the mind. This was relevant for me because my mind constantly wandered from thought to thought and jumped from desire to desire. If I was to rely solely upon my own mind to learn and practice yoga discipline, it would have been like asking a wolf to guard my sheep.

There are many different yoga teachers and schools to choose from. Each has a unique style and interpretation of yoga with varying emphasis. For example, some teachers and schools focus on yoga applications for health and body maintenance while others direct a student toward peace of mind and yoga's peak experience. Different teachers have differing personalities, teaching methods and recommended yoga practices.

A prospective student is best served when a teacher or school of yoga suits his/her needs, taste and temperament. I did not consciously search for a teacher. Finding one happened synergistically. The swami first came to my attention in a poster. I later attended one of his lectures and then offered to host him at my home. Once we got to know one another I could see that we had several interests in-common. For example, we both liked old cars, salsa and drum music, as well as discussing politics. We also shared a continuing interest in the creation of alternative communities.

I was comfortable with the swami as my teacher because his advice and teaching was clear, simple and made sense. Increasing interaction with him over the years led me to trust and love him like a family member. After a while I perceived him to be a yoga *master* and wanted to adopt him as my *guru*.

A knowledgeable adept is called a *master*. This refers to a person who has attained control over the body and mind. The highest degree of mastery attends a person who experiences an epiphany with the realization that he or she is neither the body nor the mind. When this happens, there is recognition of oneself as a nameless, formless embodiment of eternal joy. This epiphany is so intense that the realization becomes permanent. Irrespective of day-to-day situations, a yoga master lives moment-to-moment with a tranquil and joyous mind.

A master's guidance can provide a fast-track for people who would like to gain control over the mind. A living master can offer inspiration as a model of yoga practice and an example of benefits that accrue. He or she can also help students avoid or overcome pitfalls along the way.

Because masters have met with success in disciplining their minds and bodies, some have heightened perceptive abilities. This allows them to identify, diagnose and treat a student's emotional dysfunction, ill health and other impediments to self-growth and awareness.

When students decide to trust and unconditionally accept a master's help, they can adopt him/her as their teacher who thereafter is called their *guru*.

A realized master will never claim to be one. Most people who practice yoga do not have or need to take a master as a guru because they do not intend to attain its end state of samadhi. Indeed, most current public attention is not on the ultimate goal of yoga but upon its applications for wellness and stress reduction.

When I decided that Swami Satchidananda should be my guru for yoga, I took his *mantra* initiation. My ceremony for this took place in San Francisco in a converted bedroom at the Integral Yoga Institute, Balboa Street teaching center. I walked alone into a dimly lit room where Swami Satchidananda sat cross-legged on the floor in front of an altar with a photo of his teacher, flowers, a candle, a camphor lamp, incense, fruits, sweets and a small water vessel. I sat behind him as he performed a ceremony called a *puja*. This included lighting the candle, chanting, and waving the lamp. He then turned and gently cast flower petals around the room and placed one on my head. He sprinkled me with water infused with his energy and blessings.

After the puja was over, the swami gave me a personal *mantra* which was a melodic combination of Sanskrit words for use in silent meditation. Then he gave me a sweet to eat from the altar and this concluded the initiation ceremony. Two years later I received a second initiation as one of his first seven Integral Yoga Ministers.

The first 7 ministers of Integral Yoga at Initiation by Swami Satchidananda

Before my initiation, I called my mentor Swamiji. Afterwards I addressed him as *Gurudev*. My teacher received his formal name, Satchidananda from his teacher when he took initiation to become a swami. Likewise, I received a Sanskrit name when I took my guru's mantra initiation.

The swami typically gave names to his initiates. The names were related to aspects of yoga practice or selected from the pantheon of Hindu deities. I had mixed emotions when Gurudev gave me the name *Ishwara*. I secretly wanted to be named *Krishna* because I liked reading stories about him along with his alter-ego *Arjuna* who was the central figure of the Indian scripture, the *Bhagavad Gita*. Tales about Krishna described him as a charismatic and attractive figure that had many female admirers and loved to play the flute. This type of image appealed to me. *Supposedly* not knowing my preference, Gurudev chose to name me *Ishwara*. I had never heard my new name before that day. Twenty years later he explained to someone, "Ish probably wanted me to call him "Krishna" but I called him "Ishwara" because I wanted him to aspire to something higher."

When I discovered the meaning of my new name I was somewhat overwhelmed. One definition is "creator and controller of the universe". The Judeo-Christian equivalent would be "God". This name carried such great power and meaning that it seemed hard to live up to. The name both intimidated and empowered me. It suddenly presented a formidable challenge together with energized motivation to work on my life-long lack of assertiveness and low self-esteem.

The name I received from the swami also resulted in his affectionate sounding nickname for me, *Ish*. Since I never had a middle name or a nickname, this endearment also helped to improve my sense of identity and self-esteem. Gurudev usually addressed me this way, making me feel comfortable, appreciated and loved.

When I chose to become a student of Swami Satchidananda and he became my guru, my life was revolutionized and has never been the same since.

## 17 ∞ DARKNESS TO LIGHT ∞

Moving From Darkness to Light at Yogaville West *

The Sanskrit term *guru* is translated as *remover of darkness.* It can refer to a teacher of any subject who helps people overcome their limitations. Acting in such a role, Swami Satchidananda subtly encouraged me to become a more mature adult.

Reaching the age of adulthood does not guarantee independent thinking and maturity. During our youth many of us received guidance of mixed value from parents and school teachers. On one hand, it helped us to acquire skills, acculturate and prepare us for independent living. On the other hand, their training sometimes also cultivated mistaken beliefs, prejudices and limitations on imagination and creativity.

The artificial boundaries instilled by parent and school teacher training results in limitations on the breadth of our thinking, how we reason, what we believe and how we behave as adults. The influential behavior of some parents and teachers presented us with flawed or inappropriate models of how to interact with others and how we see ourselves.

Psychologists have long recognized that childhood experiences and training can trigger or cause temporary or permanently entrenched traumatic stress syndromes, rebellion, withdrawal, depression, passive-aggressive behaviors and a rather lengthy list of other minor and major personality dysfunctions that can continue into adulthood.

If and when people recognize their dysfunctional aspects and decide to address them, they typically consult a mental health professional for therapy and some are given medications. Yoga can be employed as a complementary therapy or an alternative. It is known to be helpful in stress and pain reduction as well as the resolution of emotional balance. Yoga practices can be tailored for a specific individual to address particular emotional or physical maladies.

A yoga guru can intervene as an intuitive specialist by using yoga practices to offer support and therapy for healing and growth. Outcomes can be good if the guru is trusted and recommendations are fully implemented. Tools of the guru include but are not limited to: advice, inspiration, specific yoga practices, role modeling and energy transference.

My emotionally distant and wary father did not relate to yoga, swamis, or gurus. He had a hard time pronouncing the name of my teacher but he intuitively recognized the important mentor-ship role that Swami Satchidananda fulfilled. When I would visit my dad, referring to Gurudev he would ask, "And how is *Uncle Yoga?*" In our Jewish family as in most of India, the title of *uncle* was one of respect and trust.

My grandmother understood my relationship with my teacher as that of a congregant and his rabbi. She was a little Jewish babushka lady from Latvia with a thick ethnic accent. When she visited me in Santa Barbara, she took a boat ride with Gurudev as pilot. It was a sunny day, the water was calm and we picnicked, laughed and explored the channel. When the day came to an end, Grandma said to me, "Oy, your rabbi is so fun loving. If I were younger, I would join his *kibbutz* myself."

The Swami & The Grandmother *

After Gurudev became my mentor, both my father and grandmother approved of the relationship when they noticed positive changes in my behavior and disposition. These outer signs of refinement were reflective of the inner movement from darkness to light catalyzed by my guru.

## 18 ∞ **WISE OLD MAN** ∞

Wise Old Man with Not-So-Wise Younger Man

Most indigenous cultures have a *wise man* (or woman) tradition. Throughout history, gurus, shamans, clergy, prophets, medicine men, and tribal elders fulfilled therapeutic roles. Due to their experience, self-discipline, knowledge and seniority they were able to give advice, catalyze healing or spur transformation of those who sought their help. These teacher/healers and their words were respected and heeded.

In most contemporary Western cultures the influence and healing of masters, teachers, ministers, shamans, elders or gurus is nonexistent. Media figures giving advice such as Dr. Phil, Oprah, sports figures, rock stars, movie celebrities and characters like Yoda (A take-off on yoga?) have replaced them. Other than media personalities, our closest proxies for tribal elders might be health professionals or respected relatives.

According to Jungian psychology the collective unconscious permeating all cultures throughout the history of humankind contains an archetype of the "wise old man" (or woman). Jungians believe that there is a natural need and use for this kind of trusted mentor. Faux wisdom dispensed by contemporary celebrities does not adequately fill the void left by the absence of the genuine wise old man archetypal figure. This void might be partially responsible for undeniable dysfunction in our culture such as corrupt manipulated politics, drugs, crime, greed, fraud, social injustice, suicide and international conflict. These issues persist because there is the missing element of the voice of wisdom to speak with authority in our culture as might be represented by the "wise old man". This lack of wisdom renders many parents and teachers ineffective in guiding our children into mature adulthood with the ability to live harmoniously and contribute to the building of a humane society.

The underlying purpose of a "wise old man" is to put us permanently in touch with our own inner wisdom. The teachings of Swami Satchidananda are helpful in this regard. He emphasized that the cause of social and individual ills is undisciplined egos and selfish thinking. He viewed them as primary obstacles to self-knowledge and community well-being.

When I reached "adulthood" my irresponsible habits, asocial behavior and anxieties evidenced a lack of true maturity. Realizing this, I had the choice to calcify, regress or heal and continue growing and improving. My choice was to improve by heeding the words of my mentor.

My wise old swami taught that life is best lived with decisions and actions guided by listening to the inner voice which is my inner "wise old man". Some called this concept "the guru in you".

In his talks, Swami Satchidananda said that the trustworthy inner voice in everyone is often obscured by ego-driven selfish thinking that breeds unbeneficial attitudes and self-defeating actions that can be harmful to others. He advocated introspection and meditation as ways to penetrate such mental filters so that one can benefit from the pristine guidance of intuition. I felt that following the swami's advice might enable me to be in direct and constant touch with my inner voice. This seemed like a promising path toward my goal of bathing in the calm clear lake that offered me peace, love, joy and light.

My mentor asserted that selfish thinking and concerns about self-image generate anxiety, desire, disappointment, tension, fear and a host of other such emotions. He said that they alienate an individual from his or her true nature and inner voice. Gurudev explained that every person has an underlying peaceful and loving nature with the potential of consistently experiencing bliss and joy. I understood him to say that yoga practice can empower us to moderate, transform or disassociate from an unchecked ego that generates selfish desires which in-turn alienate us from our inner wise man.

Most world religions are in agreement that undesirable actions and emotions such as theft and envy are born of selfishness and self-interest. These afflictions are sometimes called "sins". They prevent an individual from experiencing the personality, joy and inner wisdom associated with the concept of "God". Yoga philosophy agrees with such teachings and cautions that selfish acts that are hurtful to others prevent the experience of the inner voice and self realization, which I recognize as the *inner wise old man*.

The tale of Adam and Eve in paradise is an example of a biblical commentary about the hazards of self-centered desires and the way it impacts the experience of inner wisdom and joy. Yogis might interpret the biblical tale to be a warning that our perpetual experience of inner wisdom and a blissful paradise is lost when self-indulgent cravings for temporary physical and ego gratifications emerge. The biblical snake enticing Adam and Eve to lust after the forbidden apple symbolizes our undisciplined egos that drive our selfish desires. Some yoga practices are designed to tame the snake and access the realm of the inner wise old man.

## 19 ∞ EGODECTOMY ∞

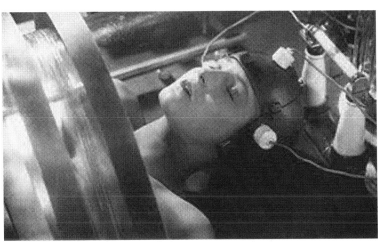

Sci-fi Version of an Egodectomy

Swami Satchidananda seemed to have a magical ability to help almost anyone get through mental and emotional blockages preventing healthy relaxed bodies, peaceful minds, inner wisdom and a paradise-like experience. He did so by employing some of his unique stealthy therapies that had the ability to treat personality disorders.

The swami believed that the root cause of personal misery, anxiety and misfortune was an overactive mind filled with self-centered or selfish perspectives due to undisciplined egos. Conversely, he maintained that selflessness is the primary determinate of personal happiness.

The ego in our active minds is a necessary part of our existence that contributes colorful veneers of motivation and personality. When healthy it is beneficial but when unhealthy it generates a fog that obscures our natural peaceful and joyful state of mind.

When egos grow too large or too small, minds become preoccupied with self-centered thoughts about superiority, inferiority, gain or loss. This results in anxiety, desire and a restless mind. Goal attainment driven by this kind of fixation is like eating candy. There is a temporary satisfaction that quickly dissipates, followed by recurring desires to get more candy. Selfish actions due to ego-centered motivations are not only self-defeating for the individual but may also victimize others and ultimately yield boomerang negative consequences.

In public appearances Gurudev would jokingly mention that he gave some students "ego-dectomies". In other words, he intentionally interacted with them in ways that they were challenged to objectively perceive and reduce their self-centered egoistic behaviors. Unknowingly, I was one of his "patients".

Before meeting my mentor, I was an anxious person with out-of-whack traits triggered by an inverted ego prompting thoughts of low self-esteem. My arrogance, self importance, and selfishness were unconscious attempts to compensate for my sense of inadequacy.

Gurudev approached my egoism in a surprising way. He did not overtly deal with it in a head-on fashion. Instead, he advised, complimented, teased or humiliated me, subtly and gently arresting my self-centered fixations. He was successful in prompting me to introspect about my sense of inadequacy and its resulting lust for being important, craving admiration from others along with status-seeking wealth and "success".

I had been suffering from relentless compulsions to overachieve in the attempt to compensate for nagging self-doubt instilled by a parent who never approved of anything that I did. This left me feeling that whatever decision I made was either wrong, inadequate or inconsequential. For example, the day that I graduated with an MBA degree, my father did not congratulate me. To fill the silence, I asked him what line of work he had expected that I would be doing. He replied with a chuckle, "A hamburger flipper."

On the day I received a PhD diploma my dad did not bother to attend graduation, yet his attitude toward me lingered-on in how I viewed my accomplishment. I took his place by considering myself to be a fake, a fraud and a phony who had tricked the faculty into conferring this honor upon me.

Lack of familial validation during my early years obviously had an erosive effect on me. The swami must have detected my upside-down ego and mounted a subtle campaign to remedy my condition by lavishing me with recognition and affection. He often validated me by asking for my advice and trusting me with important administrative decisions for his organization.

Although I was unaware of it, my teacher took on the role of a supportive surrogate father figure who approved of me to help build my self-confidence, repair my damaged ego and shed my sense of inferiority. My decades-old deep reservoir of self-doubt slowly drained away exposing an underlying bedrock of self-confidence and decisiveness. As a result, I began to love and appreciate myself. These new feelings reduced my desire for external validation, leaving me happy instead of in a state of constant self-doubt and clamoring for the approval of others.

Gurudev helped me develop a healthy self-image by validating and respecting me. This taught me the importance of doing the same for others. Thus, I learned from his example that unconditional love and acceptance is contagious. The Golden Rule is always good advice: "Love thy neighbor as thyself" but for some people like myself that lacked self-esteem, the Golden Rule also could be turned around to read, "Love thyself as thy neighbor."

The swami's therapy registered lasting results with my chronic affliction of low self-esteem. Even so, a trace of subconscious guilt still remained. Once, when flying with Gurudev to Santa Barbara, I mentioned my concern about past misdeeds and wondered if it was responsible for some of my lingering anxiety and fears of death. I asked about this issue. He turned and gazed out of the window and seemed uncharacteristically irritated as he brusquely retorted, "We can deal with these things after we land." My teacher never answered me and I didn't ask again because my anxiety and irrational fear mysteriously and permanently vanished at the end of that flight.

In Gurudev's interactions with people, he always took the opportunity to instruct, heal or help. Each person had a different need and he treated them accordingly. A word, a look, a friendly informal conversation, straight forward advice, work assignments, humiliation, scolding, abundant praise were all learning situations that were helpful for his students in promoting their growth by modifying their behavior and attitudes.

My teacher was a master psychologist cloaked in the robes of a swami. Although he joked about giving egodectomies, his whole purpose was driven by love and his mission never digressed from helping people heal from suffering, sorrow and disorder. He had a seemingly magical intuition that allowed him to recognize any pain inside a person and bring order out of chaos with his egodectomies.

## 20 ∞ PORTABLE PERSONAL GURU ∞

Swami Satchidananda Meditating at Yogaville West *

The year that I met the swami and started practicing yoga I also graduated with an advanced degree and wanted to take a trip to Europe on *Peoples Airways* that had low cost non-stop transatlantic flights. On the departure morning there was barely time to shower, have a cup of coffee grab my knapsack throw in a toothbrush and my least soiled shirt and dash to the airport.

Arriving at the airport just minutes prior to take-off was not a problem back then because there was no airport security and People's Airlines did not have ticket counters. There was just enough time to show my passport and board the plane. After it took-off an attendant came through the aisles collecting fares of $250 in cash. When the flight arrived at Gatwick I went to UK customs and at the inspector's request threw my limp knapsack on his counter. He withdrew the only item which was my displeasingly aromatic shirt and held it up, exclaiming, "You've got to be kidding!" I quickly replied, "Think of all the English clothes to buy on London's Carnaby Street!" He grunted, waving me through and mumbled, "Quite right - on with you, then!"

One night and one day in London before moving on provided inadequate time to resolve my jet lag. Travelling by train and ferry to the continent on the following morning, a group of jolly students heading for their friends in Hamburg invited me along and I made the mistake of joining them.

Hamburg and its weather proved to be grey and dreary. I was still jet-lagged and had little in common with my travel mates and their hosts who were quite a bit younger than me. No one else in town seemed to speak English and this made me feel all alone. Feeling isolated in Germany with jet lag, I started obsessing about unresolved issues back at home and remembering stories of the Holocaust. As my depression increased I resolved to leave Germany immediately.

After my first night in Hamburg I boarded a train for Amsterdam. When it eventually crossed the Dutch border, there was a beautiful sunset that seemed to promise better things. Arriving at Amsterdam Centraal, I learned that my girlfriend who was supposed to join me missed her charter flight and her ticket was no longer valid. This added to the effects of my jet lag and state of disorientation. By that time, it was dark and the shops were closed. I stood inside a store vestibule and wondered what to do and where to go and instinctively started to think about my mentor and chant his name. This made me feel a little better. Walking out of the vestibule I immediately spied a posted flyer advertising *"Meditation Room Cosmos –Open All Night".* This sounded like a good place to ground myself with some peaceful meditation.

My destination turned out to be a Dutch style coffee shop playing rock music. A meditation room was nowhere to be found. The menu offered beverages, sandwiches, pastries, marijuana and hashish. Meditation Room Cosmos turned out to be a hangout for young people sponsored by the city to keep them off the streets and out of trouble at night. As I sat down a Cosmos waitperson provided me with directions to a youth hostel, a sandwich and an excellent cup of Dutch hot chocolate with foam on top.

Looking around, I noticed a large photo of none other than Swami Satchidananda on the wall! When I asked about it, the manager said, "We don't know who this man is but the photo was here when we took over this place. We liked it so much that we left it up for ambience." I gazed at it for about 15 minutes. The familiar visage mitigated my feelings of isolation and depression. It startled me when the photo spoke and said "Go upstairs".

At the top of the stairs was a gymnasium with about 40 young Dutch men and women standing around as soft music played. Shortly after I entered, a group leader appeared and started to lead a non-verbal exercise. He told everyone to walk around for five minutes with their eyes closed. After a while we were instructed to open our eyes and stand in one place. I found myself looking directly into the eyes of a young woman. The leader then told everyone to stay in place in silence for another 5 minutes. When the silence ended it felt as though I had known this person for a long time.

After the group leader finally permitted talking, my stare-partner introduced herself as Carla. When the session ended, we went back downstairs to the Cosmos, ordered hot chocolate, and talked about yoga and the mysterious photo that had sent me upstairs. As a result, Carla became curious about the swami and this thing called yoga.

I purchased and gave my new friend one of the few yoga books printed in Dutch titled *Autobiografie van een yogi* by Paramahansa Yogananda. After reading it, she was inspired to join a hatha yoga class. I followed-up by introducing Carla to meditation and yogic breathing. She reported that all of this was helping her feel more optimistic and less depressed. My mood and outlook also brightened from having the opportunity to serve Carla by teaching what little yoga I knew at the time.

After returning from Europe I never expected to see Carla again but some weeks later, she came to the US and joined my teacher's yoga institute in Berkeley. She wanted to learn as much as she could about Gurudev's Integral Yoga®. Months later Carla returned to the Netherlands, as a professional yoga instructor and eventually became an associate of a well known European yoga master.

Before my European journey I attended many of my teacher's talks and valued his advice about how to refine myself and help others. Alone and distressed in Amsterdam, I discovered that it was possible to access the same wisdom without being in the swami's presence. Just thinking about him gave me the ability to listen to my own inner voice and tap into his advice. This became my portable personal guru.

*The teacher may not always be present, but the teaching will always be there. The teaching is the Guru. With the help of the teaching, you will realize your own Guru within. And that Guru constantly guides you in all your efforts in life. The external Guru is there to point out the Guru within you.*

*–Swami Satchidananda*

## 21 ∞ MANY PATHS TO ONE TRUTH ∞

Swami Satchidananda hosts an Interfaith Ceremony

The San Francisco counter-cultural millue of the 60s and 70s was a pronounced departure from previous norms. The psychedelic drugs commonly available in the Haight Ashbury gave many young people a taste of consciousness beyond what they knew in their former white bread suburban life.

Some in the counter-cultural community realized that there was a down side to "tripping" on substances and began to seek elevated consciousness using safe methods. As a result, intense interest mushroomed in all varieties of yoga, Buddhism, Hinduism, Sufism, esoteric Christianity and mystical Judaism. Masters of these traditions regularly came to San Francisco to share their knowledge with the burgeoning, enthusiastic counter-cultural movement. Swami Satchidananda was one such teacher that came to lecture in the Bay Area and when he did, he attracted a following in the thousands.

During those early years, the students of Swami Satchidananda in San Francisco often went as a group to learn from other teachers drawn to the new spiritual Mecca by the Bay. I also spent time on my own with the Sufi master Pir Valayit Khan, a Jewish rabbi, and Swami Muktananda who was appearing with Ram Dass, and Swami Kriyananda who was affiliated with the Self Realization Fellowship. I also attended Catholic Church masses and Protestant services and started listening to bluegrass gospel music all the time.

Within ten months of starting yoga classes I no longer was an atheist and developed an appreciation of all religions. I even became a born again Christian through the agency of a evangelical woman who had me swear on the bible as I was waiting for a Greyhound bus in Richmond, CA.

I put up a picture of Jesus on my mantle at home. When my Jewish friend came over he became quite upset about the picture and enquired in a reproachful tone, "Is that a picture of Christ on your fireplace?" I replied, "That is a picture of *Rebbe Joshu Ben Josef.* Jesus was Jewish." My friend then stormed out of my home murmuring, "I am going to ask my Rabbi about this!"

My encounter with different teachers taught me many valuable things. Even so, I was not always comfortable with their methods, teachings or personalities. After a year of sampling teachers I chose to stick with Swami Satchidananda whose teachings and presentation aligned well with my capacity, personality and temperament. I considered it to be a bonus to know that my teacher respected and participated in ceremonies and dialogue with some of the other teachers that I had known.

On the East Coast, Gurudev appeared in interfaith ceremonies with a Zen Roshi, Rabbi Joseph Gelberman, and Brother David, a Benedictine monk. When on the West Coast, the swami regularly appeared at the famous and well attended *Holy Man Jams* which featured presentations and ceremonies with 6 or more teachers from diverse esoteric traditions.

Holy Man Jam Participants Steve Gaskin, Yogi Bhajan & Swami Satchidananda

Swami Satchidananda got on well with every personality and leader that he met. During a trip to Russia, I accompanied him to a private tea reception in his honor hosted by the Prelate of the Russian Orthodox Church at his residence. The conversation was friendly with occasional eruptions of laughter. My teacher commented afterward that there had been many points of agreement between the two of them.

The swami respected agnostic and atheistic persuasions as much as religious beliefs. During the cold war, in a Soviet Russian museum a tour guide mentioned that as a communist she was not a believer. He asked her if she believed in love, kindness and comradeship. She replied, "Yes, of course." Gurudev commented, "I see, then you are a believer." On other Europe trips Gurudev met with the Pope at the Vatican.

Swami Satchidananda and Pope John Paul II at the Vatican 1984

The swami often invited clerics and monks of various religions to participate in interfaith ceremonies, symbolizing that the scriptures of seemingly divergent religions are essentially in agreement.

During the years that my teacher wintered in Santa Barbara, he spent substantial time working on a design for an inter-faith monument. He intended it as a shrine to promote awareness of the common threads and truths that run through all religions. The goal was to inspire inclusive thinking and mutual understanding between religious groups. Swami Satchidananda demonstrated his message by participating in ceremonies with clergy of many religions including Christian, Buddhist, Jain, African, Native American and Judaism.

Swami Satchidananda was resolutely intolerant of religious intolerance. The strongest remark that I ever heard him make about anything was, "If someone tells me that I will go to hell because I do not believe like him, then I will tell him to go to hell."

The swami's ability to tolerate the extremities of divergent religious views was tested during his talk at the Unitarian church in Berkeley, California. A man in the audience stood up and interrupted what Gurudev was saying as he shouted, "Jesus Christ is the only son of God. All other teachers are agents of the devil and false prophets." That evening when returning from the lecture, Gurudev confided, "Thank heaven I kept my anger in my back pocket." My resonance with my mentor grew when I realized that his unexpressed anger was a normal human response to rudeness and bigotry.

An incident at the San Francisco Airport allowed me to see another facet of Gurudev's response to religious myopia. I was one among many bidding Gurudev farewell when a Krishna Consciousness monastic approached him and offered Gurudev *prasad* which is traditional Indian sacramental food first offered to a deity, blessed and then eaten by adherents. Its function is similar to the Catholic ritual wafer. Gurudev took the morsel with a reverential attitude and swallowed. He then reached into his bag and offered his snack to the Krishna monk who refused to take it. Our teacher gently asked, "Why?" The monk replied, "The food was not blessed by Krishna." Gurudev replied, "Who do you think I am?"

Swami Satchidananda recognized, honored and celebrated all faiths no matter where or how they presented themselves. For example, on one occasion he and I approached the residence of a Native American tribal leader near Taos New México. After we crossed the threshold, Gurudev stopped and silently knelt down, bowed his head and uttered a prayer. In the corner I saw a hand-made doll tied to a twig. He had instantly perceived that it was an altar. Our Western Indian host immediately warmed to his Eastern Indian guest as a result of the swami's reverence.

My mentor's interest in encouraging understanding and harmony did not stop at identifying common threads running through all faiths. He also dialogued with scientists and emphasized the similarity between scientific discoveries and yogic thinking about life's mysteries. Gurudev believed that yoga, religion and science had more points of agreement than not. He often remarked that the existence of atoms was identified in yogic writings that dated back thousands of years.

I was present at a private meeting in Stanford University between Buckminster Fuller and the swami. They chatted for an hour over beverages and a snack. Although I did not listen to their entire conversation, of particular interest to me was their discourse about the similarity between Fuller's geodesic dome innovations and the structural elements of Gurudev's Lotus shrine

Swami Satchidananda and Buckminster Fuller at Stanford University *

At one time or another, followers of every religious faith have experienced and perpetrated discrimination, persecution and murder in the name of deity and doctrine. To encourage an end to the history of endless acrimony in the name of a god or religion, Swami Satchidananda sought to express the similarity of teachings and scripture in every known religion. To articulate the similarity, he not only conceived of a shrine symbolizing the common threads running through all religions but he also included symbols of major religions in the logo of his Integral Yoga Institute. He declared:

*TRUTH IS ONE PATHS ARE MANY*

## 22 ∞ LOTUS IN BLOOM ∞

LOTUS Shrine - Yogaville, VA

*Truth Is One Paths Are Many* was and still is the motto of interfaith initiatives of Swami Satchidananda. It became the theme for a shrine that he wanted to manifest as a symbol of the underlying unity of all religions. In designing the shrine, my teacher was influenced by his friend and admirer Mr. Mahalingum, an Indian business magnate who was dedicated to restoring ancient Indian temples for the worship of light as a symbol for the divine. Mahalingum became an important supporter of the swami's shrine and suggested using light as the central unifying theme for the interior layout.

The name given to the shrine emphasized the light symbolism: *The Light of Truth Universal Shrine.* Its initials spelled out "LOTUS" and Gurudev usually referred to it as the "Lotus Temple". The exterior architecture of the shrine was to be a pink-tinged semblance of a gigantic lotus flower. Lotus petals traditionally signify spiritual enfoldment in some Eastern cultures and they were also included as a primary element in the logo of Gurudev's Integral Yoga Institute.

The Lotus was originally planned for installation on a hill overlooking a canyon with a view clear to the ocean on 62 acres that comprised the Yogaville West community in Santa Barbara. Ironically, when our group went for a government construction permit, the proposal for a monument to the unity of all faiths met with religious intolerance. It was bitterly opposed by homeowners of a small residential tract located a mile away that contained a large percentage of fundamentalist Christian family homes. They testified and protested against the design and location of Lotus at the hearing. Gurudev attended the hearing which concluded without action pending further deliberation. I offered my professional opinion that the permit would ultimately be granted. Never-the-less Gurudev gave me instructions to immediately withdraw the permit application. He said that the Lotus would be built where neighbors would appreciate it. As a result Yogaville West in Santa Barbara which was planned as a central IYI facility and the home for the Lotus was vacated and sold.

It is notable that Gurudev's decision to not proceed with building the Lotus in Santa Barbara resulted in moving the entire community and Lotus site to Virginia. Years after the Santa Barbara Yogaville property was sold, the devastating Painted Cave brush fire roared through thousands of acres, burning hundreds of homes. If Lotus had been built on the Santa Barbara site it would have been devastated along with the Yogaville West community.

Once the replacement site for Yogaville was established, Lotus was built and became a prominent landmark in Buckingham County, located in Central Virginia.

Swami Satchidananda designed the Lotus during his winters in Santa Barbara and devoted many hours working with University of California Professor Hansma in his lab to perfect technology for the light feature of the shrine. Several lighting prototypes were tested before the design was completed. The first time that I viewed the final version of the centerpiece light model at the UC campus laboratory, I realized that Lotus was going to be something more than a mere monument. After it was erected, the Lotus had a magical other-worldly ambiance.

The exterior of Lotus was anthropomorphic, giving visitors a sense that the shrine was a living presence. The entry to the Lotus is located on the lower level and an encased winding stairway provides for ascension to the upper level which has a transformational effect upon the visitor. There is a sensation of entering a tranquil alternative universe where anxiety and emotional baggage is left behind. Part of the ambiance is achieved by the thematic lighting that Gurudev designed while in Santa Barbara. A central kinetic column of light is filled with a cloud-like substance that moves slowly upward. It emerges from a representation of a large lotus themed Yantra symbol at the base and extends to the domed ceiling. The column is reminiscent of a giant ultraviolet or florescent tube that emits an ethereal light. The light shaft splits into smaller rays that travel in different directions along a high domed ceiling following its curve down to 12 individual altars of different world religions.

LOTUS Shrine Yogaville, VA

Lotus is not only a shrine dedicated to all faiths. It is also a silent meditation chamber. It feels like being inside of a peaceful yet kinetic presence that catalyzes healing.

The shrine induces an immediate focus and a meditative response in the mind. In addition to its ecumenical symbolism, the light feature and domed architecture seems to extinguish worrisome thoughts and purify the mind and body.

During the years that I was in residence at Yogaville I lived close to the Lotus and meditated there regularly. On one occasion, instead of enjoying the tranquility I experienced troubling thoughts about an ill wife and daughter. I also started worrying about past due bills. This was indeed curious because I was not married, did not have a daughter and didn't have any unpaid bills! I realized that the thoughts that entered my mind were those of the only other visitors to Lotus on that day. I recalled that as I drove into the parking lot, a man, woman, and a child were just leaving in a rusty old station wagon. It seemed to me that the meditation chamber had absorbed the husband's worries and lingering traces were still slowly being dispersed and dissolved by the Lotus. This story is but one among many magic moments enjoyed by those who visit this iconic radiant lotus light flower.

*More people have died in the name of God and religion than in all the wars and natural calamities. But, the real purpose of any religion is to educate us about our spiritual unity. It is time for us to recognize that there is one truth and many approaches. The basic cause for all the world problems is the lack of understanding of our spiritual unity. The need of the hour is to know, respect, and love one another and to live as one global family. Our humble aim in building the LOTUS was to spread this message.*

   *-Swami Satchidananda*

## 23 ∞ NO FAITH IS AN ISLAND ∞

Kandy Sri Lanka  *

Before Swami Satchidananda immigrated to America he presided over a yoga ashram in Sri Lanka. His former home was near the town of Kandy in a region that contained beautiful hillside tea plantations. The island was an important destination for Buddhist pilgrims because Kandy hosted a temple containing a tooth from the body of The Buddha.

The purpose of our island sojourn was a visit and a talk that Gurudev had been invited to present at the Divine Life Society in Colombo. The society was an organization dedicated to the teachings of Sri Swami Sivananda who was my teacher's teacher.

While we were in Colombo we stayed at an old fashioned English luxury hotel on a waterfront bluff. There we drank coconut water out of the shell and basked in the sun at poolside. Later we went to the northern part of the island where we toured Hindu temples and visited with some of Gurudev's old friends. We also went swimming in the warm ocean water that lapped on palm lined white sandy beaches. This was delightful except for the sting ray attack that we endured.

Sri Lanka was a splendid tropical paradise but its heavenly ambiance was diminished by human acrimony. Buddhists constituted a majority on the south end of the island. Hindu Tamils located in settlements in the north were a sizable minority. Although both religions are known for pacifistic doctrines, there was tension and violent skirmishes between the two groups.

In the years following our Sri Lanka trip the island erupted into full scale civil war. Killing is always uncalled for but even more so in an island paradise inhabited by people of two pacifistic faiths. During his years on the island, Gurudev had experienced the impact of fighting between the Tamils and Buddhists. The daily toll taken by religious intolerance convinced him to become an advocate for mutual understanding and cooperation between all faiths.

After coming to America, the swami consistently encouraged ecumenism, interfaith dialogue and ceremonies. In his talks, he declared that divinity and godliness was to be found inside a person and that this could be realized through either yoga or religious practices.

My teacher kept an altar in his home with a statue of Nataraja, the dancing Hindu deity symbolizing creation and destruction cycles in the universe. On holidays he performed religious ceremonies called *pujas* that evoked deities of all religions. Although the swami was raised from birth as Tamil Hindu, he recognized the need to transcend religious doctrine in order to experience divinity and he would often proclaim, "I am not a Hindu I am an *Undo*."

My mentor was supportive of his students who were inclined to practice their birth religion in addition to yoga. He taught that religion is helpful for personal growth but for the ultimate spiritual experience, one must not be attached to anything including yoga and religion.

Although yoga and Hinduism shared the same geographical and cultural context, the origins of yoga pre-date Hinduism. The difference between yoga and Hinduism is that yoga is a collection of methods for personal growth, health and self-discovery whereas Hinduism is a faith based upon beliefs in gods and goddesses.

Although my teacher called himself an "Undo" his beard, robes and gentle demeanor made him the picture of a classical religious prophet. His inspirational sayings and writings communicated wisdom, love and compassion. Gurudev's yoga communities were home to some who chose to become monks and nuns and like him they were dedicated to the interfaith creed of their master.

*Truth is the same always. Whoever ponders it will get the same answer. Buddha got it. Patanjali got it. Jesus got it. Mohammed got it. The answer is the same, but the method of working it out may vary this way or that.*

*–Swami Satchidananda*

# 24 ∞ YOGA VILLAGE 1.0 ∞

Yogaville Lunchtime

After the Integral Yoga Institute found a permanent home in San Francisco, Swami Satchidananda and his students were intent on forming model cooperative communities based upon yogic principles. There was plenty of interest in the concept because communes were *au courant* in the counter-culture of the time. The very first Yogaville in the U.S. was established at an aging neglected former resort for Jewish vacationers from the Bay Area. It was located in Northern California and was known as Seigler Springs. There were many unique aspects to the property including several varieties of hot mineral wells, bathhouses and swimming pools, a lodge, cabins and a creek with its water temperature at 98 degrees.

Seigler Springs in Lake County, CA became the first Yogaville

Alas, the attempt to make a go of the first Yogaville was to be unsuccessful. The aged sewage system failed shortly after we acquired the property. To replace it would have required a massive infusion of cash greater than our meager funds. The failure occurred during a crowded yoga retreat with Gurudev in attendance for Christmas and New Year festivities.

The sewage retention pond overflowed because of system failure compounded by a high transient population due to the holiday events. Things then went from bad to worse. Our chief maintenance person tried to remedy the situation by turning some valves but there was extreme cold that evening and he slipped on ice, lost a finger in the process and landed in the sewage pond. When the pond continued to overflow a decision was made to distribute the effluent on the adjacent vacant acreage using a high pressure pump and fire hoses. The next morning, we woke to see the trees on our neighbor's property festively decorated for the holidays with our frozen used toilet paper that evidenced the previous night's sewage relocation. That incident is one example of a multitude of problems that descended to make life difficult for Yogaville residents.

Another problem was the discomfort of female community members due to the presence of a ghost. This problem raised so much concern that when Gurudev came to visit, there was a special assembly during which time he told the members how to deal with and banish the unwanted apparition. His advice was simply to sternly tell the errant spirit that it was not wanted and to "go away".

The first Yogaville did not have a long life. A contributing factor was that most community members did not want to work at outside jobs to pay for the expenses of daily operations and upgrades needed by the community. As a result of the financial constraints community meals were marginal. I recall one lunch that only consisted of very watery turnip and kale soup. The snowy cold and windy climate in the winter at the Northern California mountain location was not hospitable. Inadequate heating combined with a minimal fuel budget made for uncomfortable living arrangements.

The final straw for Yogaville came when its director was forced to resign because of his wife's demands to abandon the miserable conditions. At the time, I was residing 600 miles away in warm and comfortable San Diego. Gurudev called me and told me of the resignation and said, "The people at Yogaville just want to sit there and meditate. They do not want to take financial responsibility for their home." He inquired if I would be interested in replacing the departing director and instituting financial reorganization. I respectfully declined because I wanted to retain my university professorship. He then said, "Sell it!"

Selling the property was not a pleasant experience. I did not like to see our community come to this end. I dutifully advertised the Yogaville property and after a long time there was a nibble. I negotiated the sale with people who scared me silly. They identified themselves as "disciples of Da Free John" (formerly Franklin Jones, he later renamed himself Adi Da). He had been a former student of Swami Muktananda who wrote a book about what he called *spiritual materialism*. Some of his followers wore dark suits, sunglasses and carried what looked to me like firearms. They were not adverse to employing pressure and intimidation in their negotiations with me. They purchased the property and fenced it off to the public. There was a rumor that armed guards were posted at the entrance. They renamed the resort and sunk ten million dollars into redevelopment. Its name changed over the intervening years but not its ownership.

The first Yogaville was gone but its spirit lived-on. Like the phoenix it was destined to be reborn out of the ashes in one of the most beautiful places in the entire world.

## 25 ∞ YOGA IN PARADISE ∞

Proposed Santa Barbara Lotus Site - The Hills Were Alive With the Sound of Om-Music

By 1974, the thriving urban California Integral Yoga Institutes that offered yoga classes formulated by Swami Satchidananda had been established in San Francisco, Los Angeles, Berkeley and Santa Cruz. There was also a natural food store owned by the IYI in Santa Cruz. Residents living in the institutes taught daily classes to non-residential students. Well attended yoga retreats featuring Gurudev were held during winter months in California. At the time our teacher was living in Connecticut and New York City. Because he was accustomed to the warm weather in Sri Lanka, the swami found it desirable to visit his California institutes in the winter months. During this time he would meet with students, appear in large yoga retreats and give public talks.

When the swami visited the Los Angeles Integral Yoga Institute one of the residents named Shankar suggested a trip to Santa Barbara and my teacher agreed. I drove to meet Gurudev and Shankar for a several day stay in Santa Barbara in my 1951 gold colored Hudson Hornet that looked like an overturned bathtub. Gurudev requested that we tour the town in my ancient auto and noted, "Your car is so strong that an elephant can walk over it." He insisted upon driving it all the time and named the vehicle "Ganesh" after the elephant god. Shankar was also impressed and within months he acquired a similar purple colored automotive relic of his own. I encouraged him to name it "Shan-Car" but to no avail. The three of us delighted in the palm tree lined pristine beaches accented by Spanish architecture and mountains in a lush land with the best climate in the US. I found it hard to leave Santa Barbara when our brief visit came to a close. At the time, I would never have guessed that I would return and live there.

I was working in San Diego and living in a home that I had just purchased. Three months after I moved-in, Gurudev called me and said, "Ish, let's start a yoga community in Santa Barbara." That weekend I went up to Santa Barbara to look for property for the proposed community and for a residence that would accommodate my teacher. I knew that locating a yoga community there would keep him in Santa Barbara for several winter months of each year. I wanted a house with a living room large enough to hold community meetings with Gurudev and I found just such a place.

I found a four-bedroom home on a half-acre that was situated directly on a bluff with ocean frontage. It also had a maid's quarters with a second kitchen and a separate entrance. The house had been built for and lived in by an 89 year old woman named Rose who was born and raised in Germany. She had never seen the inside of a hospital or had a sick day in her life and attributed her good health to the fact that she had been a vegetarian since birth. Because of this her house never had meat in its kitchen. The name of the street was appropriate for Gurudev. It was located on *El Camino De La Luz* which means "road of the light". Many of Gurudev's students considered him to be their guru which means "remover of darkness". Furthermore, he had intended to build *The Light of Truth Universal Shrine.*

Everything was perfect about the house on the ocean bluff except for one thing. The purchase required more down payment money than I had. Within days of finding the perfect house, a fellow yoga student by the name of Allison called me out of the blue and said, "I understand that you are trying to find a home to accommodate Gurudev. If you need some funds, I can loan you the money. I have up to $20,000 available." That sum of cash was *exactly* the amount I needed and the home was purchased!

For eight months of each year my new Santa Barbara home was my residence. During the other four winter months that Gurudev lived there, it was necessary to make room for him by moving into the maid's quarters. I worked three days a week as a professor in San Diego and commuted back and forth to serve the swami in Santa Barbara for the balance of the week. Every Saturday night, the local yoga students and those from Los Angeles would come to my house to be with our teacher. Over 120 people squeezed-in and sat on the floor of the living room for a meeting with Gurudev.

For two years from the time that our teacher arrived in Santa
Barbara we looked for a suitable spot to plant the proposed yoga
community. When Gurudev was not otherwise occupied, he enjoyed
relaxing outside my house in the back yard, watching whales cruising
by as he sat in an ugly chaise lounge that had the uncanny look of a
giant green vinyl alligator. A fellow yoga student who was a
contractor built a private stairway down the steep cliff so that
Gurudev could access the beach below.

There was a constant stream of visitors to see Gurudev at El
Camino De La Luz. The famous singer/composer Carol King also
visited occasionally and took walks with Gurudev on the beach. Carol
had been given the name *Karuna* (Goddess of Mercy) by Gurudev
when she was initiated. She had become a yoga instructor at
Gurudev's yoga institute in Los Angeles. One afternoon, Gurudev
presided over a private wedding in the living room at El Camino Del
La Luz between long time yoga student, attorney Dhivya Goldman
and famed folk guitarist John Fahey.

In spite of the incredible bluff-front charm of my house, Gurudev
did not relish the idea living at the ocean. Toward the end of his third
winter in Santa Barbara, a home in the hills of nearby Montecito was
purchased for his exclusive use which he named *La Paz* (The Peace).

Gurudev seemed to love his new home located high in the hills of
Montecito. The terrain was reminiscent of the land near his former
Sri Lanka home. His site had a commanding view of the village below
and the Pacific Ocean. The home was a modest two bedroom with

just room enough to accommodate Gurudev and his assistant.

During his years wintering in Montecito Gurudev became a fan of the Rose Bowl Parade in Pasadena. Every New Years day my phone would ring and my teacher would be on the line giving an enthusiastic review and commentary about the festive floats.

Swami Satchidananda at La Paz

A fellow student came from San Francisco to visit the master. He and I purchased and installed a spa for Gurudev to soak in at La Paz. A room was built around the spa and it became a place that our teacher retreated to almost every evening. During the installation the Swami oversaw our work, often criticizing what we were doing. I considered this part of our learning process to minimize our egos.

While in residence at La Paz, the Swami went to the local pound and adopted what must have been the two most unattractive and unwanted old dogs in the continental US: a male and female that he named *Sita* and *Ram* after the Hindu deity couple. A full time maintenance person who was a yoga student lived in a small travel trailer at the property edge to help with the grounds and security

In Santa Barbara the swami made friends from all walks of life. A spiritually inclined real estate appraiser who was a recovering alcoholic often spent time with him. They would meet at the beach and ride horses bareback along and through the surf. A couple who owned a hobby shop got Gurudev interested in building and flying model airplanes. They kept in touch with him on a CB radio and met him every week along with other model plane enthusiasts in a vacant field for a flight-fest. Once a week, Gurudev would visit their hobby shop and spend time examining and tinkering with their products and displays.

Many yoga community members were able to join the swami at the cinema, on recreational drives and during his window shopping. They also had many opportunities to host him during scheduled and surprise visits at their homes.

The sellers of La Paz took a liking to my teacher. They came to his weekly talks. Gurudev was tickled by their bumper sticker that read, "Ignore alien orders!" and he constantly teased them about this. The couple often returned for a visit at La Paz and became fast friends with the swami. The real estate broker who handled our purchases also became a friend and admirer of our teacher. She would visit him and come to his frequent public talks in downtown Santa Barbara.

Other local friends that the swami visited included a professor of religious studies at the local university and a German car mechanic. He enjoyed going to the auto shop to discuss and monitor mechanical repairs on Aston Martins, Jaguars, Bentleys and Citroens.

When it was decided to start a yoga community in Santa Barbara, a few prospective members started to move there even before we found a permanent facility. To accommodate them, I purchased a cottage complex located on Laguna Street. This tiny enclave became the nexus of our budding community until we were able to acquire a permanent facility for the group. When my yoga friends relocated to my complex I didn't raise the rents from historical rates. My only motivation for purchasing the complex was to plant a seed to help grow a yoga community.

Two years went by and at long last, a property was identified that met our needs for the proposed community. It consisted of 62 acres with some avocados and citrus trees located in the foothills along San Marcos Pass Road. There was a hill on the property that had a view of the valley below and the ocean beyond. It had a 100 year-old farmhouse and a barn overlooking a creek. The heavenly little rural enclave felt remote but it was only 12 minutes from downtown and even closer to a regional shopping center. It had been originally built as a resting area to serve a stage coach route that ran over San Marcos Pass between Santa Barbara and points north. Gurudev became interested in this property because it was perfect for his Lotus shrine.

The price for the real estate that became Yogaville West was $125,000. I contacted four other members of the IYI and each of us donated $25,000 to purchase the property. Today the same property is worth $2,500,000.

Eventually many people migrated to Santa Barbara to join Gurudev and become part of the new yoga community. Newcomers took rentals in town and others eventually moved out to the Yogaville property. Twenty-five members were assigned to rooms in the small farmhouse, the upstairs of the old barn and an adjacent trailer. The lower level of the barn served as a gathering place. Gurudev came from La Paz on Saturday nights to give a talk. The gathering for that purpose was called a *satsang*. Several of us formed a rock and blues band to play during satsang nights. An organic farm was established along with a food distribution business intended to make money for the community. Yoga lessons were taught in town by community members.

Satsang Hall at Yogaville West Santa Barbara

I purchased property near the University of California with a falafel stand and donated its use to Yogaville as a business to make extra community income. Next to the stand I owned vacant land that was adjacent to an expanding photocopy business serving the student population. The curly haired owner of the business next door begged me to sell him my excess land to expand the parking lot for his shop which was becoming very successful. I granted his request. His nickname was "Kinko" and this property was his first store location. He later expanded into a national chain which was bought out by FedEx. I should have taken stock instead of money from Kinko!

Gurudev seemed gratified about the amount of effort expended by members to maintain and grow the second Yogaville at Santa Barbara. By then, many of its members were more responsible because they had learned important lessons from the financial failure of the previous Yogaville. The Santa Barbara community can be called successful because it thrived during its adolescence. When neighbors resisted locating the Lotus there the community was moved to Virginia and it never had the chance to fully develop.

When the decision was made to move eastward, Gurudev no longer came to Santa Barbara. He instructed me to sell the Yogaville property and his beloved La Paz. This saddened me because I had never seen my teacher as comfortable in any other place that he lived. The proceeds from the sale of Yogaville West and his home in Montecito went toward the purchase and development of the present facility known as Satchidananda Ashram - Yogaville in Buckingham County, Virginia.

## 26 ∞ PEACOCK BLISS ∞

A Proud Peacock – The 1959 Cadillac Sedan Deville

Driving through the hills of Santa Barbara one sunny afternoon became a memorable event for me. Swami Satchidananda typically treated me like a close friend but not on that day. His relatives had just flown-in from India and I assumed one of my usual roles as chauffeur/baggage handler and general flunky. On that occasion my teacher had been barking orders and criticizing everything that I did. As I was driving him and his party in his car called the *Peacock* he uncharacteristically excluded me from conversation.

I grumbled to myself. "Here I am, AA, BSc, MBA, PhD, successful business man and professor. I am carrying bags and taking abuse as though I was some sort of unpaid servant. I must be crazy, there's nothing in it for mm…........................" I could not finish the last word because my ability to think was overwhelmed by a blissful sensation. I realize that I could not add an *e* to the end of the *m* because the "*I*-dentification" of my ego dissolved in the bliss. An instant before this occurred I started to really love myself because I was doing something with a 100% pure selfless motive with no expectation of approval, appreciation or even a thank you. In the micro-moment that followed a macro-energy flash coursed up my spine and I became deliriously happy. No, not happy – but blissful. No, not blissful – but beyond that! I experienced myself as a weightless, formless, nameless, shameless and blameless entity disassociated from the body. I had expanded, elevated, and floated, losing track of my thoughts and the story line of my life with all of its trifling enjoyments and "issues".

My out-of-body experience was sublime for me but it might have been hazardous for my passengers. Fortunately, after some time the thought entered my vacated mind that "I" was still driving and needed to locate and re-enter the body and attempt to focus upon driving the Peacock. The transition was difficult after floating away like a peaceful cloud and wanting to stay that way forever. When the car ride ended it dawned upon me that my out-of-body and mind experience had been profound. But no matter, the luggage needed to be unloaded.

In the days and weeks that followed I remembered my unique experience which for public safety reasons I hoped did not often descend upon other drivers while they were on the road. Illicit substances had not been involved, so why and how had I experienced so much blissful contentment? I wanted more of that - but not particularly again while driving! Did my teacher somehow zap me with a cosmic ray? Unlikely.

I realized that inner self-approval of my motives and actions triggered the experience. I had ignored my desires in the face of criticism and continued helping others with no prospects of a reward of any kind. This occasion was the first time that I started to totally love and accept myself instead of trying to receive it from others. This kind of inner love could not be lost. I was two-in-one; father & son, mother & child, lover & beloved, god & man, heaven & earth, up & down without beginning and without end - ∞**Self-contained**∞.

My understanding of the reason for the disembodied blissed-out car driving experience was confirmed at a public talk that my teacher was giving. He explained that adopting a truly selfless attitude was the practice of *karma yoga* and it was an uncomplicated path to the benefits and goal of yoga.

After my epiphany, I consciously practiced my karma yoga but often fell short by not being aware that I was harboring selfish motives. I thereby deprived myself of that most wonderful feeling. Never-the-less, my attempts at selfless service continue until the present time. Whether or not flawed, this allows me to look in the mirror and say to myself with conviction "I love you, warts and all!"

*When you do anything and everything, do it selflessly. Do not expect anything in return; not money or praise or even a thank you. As a result you will enjoy supreme peace.*
*-Swami Satchidananda*

## 27 ∞ GOOD CAR-MA ∞

Swami Satchidananda Repairing the Peacock

The swami's 1959 Cadillac Sedan de Ville was 17 feet long and had fins as high as my shoulders complete with quadruple bullet tail lights that made it look like a turquoise rocket ship. The car had been equipped at the factory with every option including automatically dimming headlights. This veteran conveyance was purchased for the sum of $700.00 and it was my teacher's pride and joy. He called it *The Peacock*. Driving and maintaining this vehicle was a leisure-time hobby for him.

Gurudev added a citizens band radio to the Peacock. While driving it he often called me over his CB using the "handle" or code name of "Peacock". When he was out for a drive and I was in my odd-looking French Citroen, a CB call would come from him: "French frog, this is Peacock, over!" I would respond "French-frog, here, over" "French-frog, call Bad Badger and tell him I will meet him at the flight field, over and out." Thereafter Bad Badger, French

Frog and Peacock would meet at an open field in Goleta for an hour to work on and fly the radio controlled model airplane which Peacock had assembled as directed by Bad Badger who owned the local hobby shop.

The following year, my teacher changed my CB handle from *French-frog* to *French-fry* because when we dined out together he noted that deep-fried spuds were my favorite dish. The quantities that I consumed of this fat laden preparation might not have met with Gurudev's approval but he diplomatically said nothing about the matter, except to re-designate my CB handle.

Automobiles were also a "vehicle" that Gurudev used to teach and test me. On one day when Gurudev insisted that I drive at high speed I swerved to avoid a small animal on the road. I thought "Of course a man of peace would have me spare the little creature". Suddenly my teacher asked, "Are you driving to save the life of the animal or are you driving to save the life of the swami?" Then I realized that I had put our lives at risk by making a pat assumption while disregarding the resulting potential danger. This rude awakening stuck with me. After this incident I always tried to objectively evaluate each situation in my life rather than automatically acting on some politically correct assumption.

The swami owned several cars but his favorite was the *Peacock* which I found for him in Ventura. It was also my favorite. One day I found a white convertible of the same vintage as the Peacock with the same rocket ship styling. I purchased it for myself and when Gurudev came to town I proudly took him to see it. He praised its good looks and immediately said, "This would be a good car for a swami." Within days I had the interior restored and the exterior repainted and then presented it to him as a gift. This was a test to see if I was attached to my new purchase. Five weeks after I gave the convertible to Gurudev, he gave me his equally finned white 1959 Imperial hardtop with only 50,000 miles that he called *Nandi*.

Over the years in addition to the Cadillac convertible, I gave Gurudev a 1973 AMC Pacer purchased for $300, a 1959 Cadillac limousine and many other whimsical gifts and even some practical ones.

Although I never expected it, each time I gave him a gift, sooner or later Gurudev always gave back something of equal or greater value. Twenty years of hosting Gurudev at my various residences was also reciprocated. He invited me to be a permanent guest at his Virginia home. He allocated part of his guest house duplex in his personal compound to me. I stayed there for two years then he made sure that I was accommodated rent-free in a mobile home on the Yogaville campus.

In retrospect my mentor neither needed nor wanted anything from me or anyone else for that matter during the years that I was with him. Never-the-less he always gave me and others opportunities to practice selfless attitudes and motivations when helping and gifting him. This was his way of teaching about how to live every day and every moment practicing karma yoga and enjoying the resulting tranquility of mind and buoyancy of spirit.

# 28 ∞ RESPECTING WISDOM ∞

Swami Satchidananda greeted by M. Desai, the Prime Minister of India *

Gurudev enjoyed restaurant dining once a week or more when he was in Santa Barbara. He often went to a French-Italian cafe in the downtown called *Jacques*. Although the staff and maitre d' had no knowledge of who the swami was or what he did they were fascinated and charmed by him and always received him as royalty. Gurudev was seated at the best table and three waitresses would clamor to serve him. At meal's end they gathered around the table to chat with him and listen to whatever he had to say. Jacques never charged for the swami's meal.

The response to Gurudev at Jacques was one example of how people saw something special in him without even knowing who he was. This kind of reception was universal. Another example was evidenced in Russia. A group of old Babushkas were standing in front of the altar in worship when he and I entered an Orthodox church in Moscow. The swami stayed for a brief time and as he exited, the women turned from their rituals, rushed outside, and crowded around him. The babushkas did not know who he was but a few silently hugged Gurudev while others wept openly and two fell at his feet.

I witnessed another kind of reception for the swami in India. It was even more remarkable than the one in Russia. He was invited to preside at the dedication of a restored ancient temple dedicated to the worship of light that was established centuries ago by Saint Ramalinga. Our host was Mr. Mahalingum, a wealthy industrialist who had financed the temple restoration project.

We attempted to drive into the town where the temple was located but this was impossible. Our vehicle caravan had to stop when the drivers saw that the road and sidewalks were overflowing with townsfolk wanting to catch a glimpse of or receive a blessing from my teacher. In order to get through to the dedication site, our party had to dismount from our cars and walk several blocks through the throng. Many people in the street tried to touch Gurudev's garment while others shouted out requests for blessings or healings. Townsfolk also grabbed at my garments, pleading for boons.

I knew that many Indian people respected and revered men and women who were known as masters or gurus but the intensity and drama of the townsfolk in approaching my teacher was a novel experience for me. The scene that day must have been similar to what the disciples of Jesus witnessed when their master walked from place to place to teach and heal. It felt as though I had stepped into a scene right from the bible

Our party consisted of the swami and his host accompanied by
two of his driver/bodyguards with some of Gurudev's yoga students.
As we walked through the crowd, people fell at his feet. In India,
prostrating in front of a person is a sign of respect shown many
different teachers, family members and public figures. Although this
was not a requirement, some of Gurudev's American students did
occasionally bow and touch his feet.

When the villagers tried to fall at his feet, my teacher passively and
kindly received the honor. One time after several people had gone
through their gestures, he turned to me and remarked, "They may
bow at my feet today but what will they do tomorrow? I would rather
that they follow my advice than fall at my feet."

Gurudev never insisted that his followers practice self-
subordination in his presence, however, bowing was included in
traditional puja ceremonial rituals that were part of festive events at
his Yogaville.

The day after the Indian light temple dedication, our party visited
the ashram of Swami Chidbhavananda who had been one of
Gurudev's earliest teachers. Upon arrival, Gurudev first touched and
then sat at the feet of his host. I usually saw my teacher as the center
of attention and respect but in this case, he completely subordinated
himself. It was a memorable scene as my mentor who was an
international celebrity reverted to the role of a contented young boy
demonstrating heartfelt silent respect in the presence of one of his
former teachers

Gestures or rituals outwardly signifying humility in the presence of a master are not a necessary part of being a yoga student. Even so, in some respects, it couldn't hurt.

There is a cultural dimension to bowing and/or touching the feet of another person. In some Asian countries this is an acceptable and often expected way to greet a friend, relative, teacher or important visitor. On a mundane level it is similar to shaking hands or giving a hug. On a deeper level these greeting conventions can be a sign of heart-felt affection, respect or recognition of the divine presence in another person. Some American yoga students and practitioners adopt these customs when they choose to embrace aspects of the Indian culture that birthed yoga. Others choose the conventions because they feel a need to "fit-in" due to peer pressure.

Ego containment plays a significant role in yoga practice. Symbolically subordinating oneself can be helpful in deflating an oversized ego and conditioning the mind to respect other people and cultivate self respect. This is why humility gestures are associated with engendering a worshipful attitude for the practice of bhakti yoga. Finally, a humble mind can accept beneficial energy flows from teacher to student. The nature and dynamics of that energy flow is described in the following chapter.

# 29 ∞ CONTAGIOUS ENERGY ∞

I once had a private meeting with Gurudev during a yoga retreat in the beautiful redwood covered hills of Santa Cruz. He was relaxing on a large wicker chair with his bare feet stretched before him. I entered his room and instinctively bowed and touched them. Immediately, an inner tranquility overtook my mind and my body seemed weightless.

The peaceful powerful energy that passed from Gurudev to me at the retreat sometimes occurs between a master and anyone who approaches with a humble attitude. This dynamic was what my hippie friends described as a "contact high". The energy that flows between people is called *prana* or *Shakti*.

Every living body is continually energized by its own internal prana. There is also typically latent but powerful prana stored in the body at the base of the spine. This is sometimes referred to as *kundalini* energy and when it is stimulated and unleashed it travels upward through the spine to the head. Like many others, I experienced mild kundalini energy surges long before practicing yoga. When I felt inspired, elated or scared I got chills up my spine. Many teens had similar experiences while watching "B" rated movies of the 1950s advertised as "spine tingling".

If a toxin-free body is relaxed and the mind is not obsessed with self-concerns or if prana is transferred from a master, a person's latent internal spinal energy can spontaneously move up the spine. When this happens, the energy rises through and adds charges to a hierarchy of individual nodes or centers in the body along the spine called *chakras*. Lower chakras are associated with energy for managing basic animal needs and desires of humans such as survival and procreation. Higher chakras relate to refined human characteristics such as love. The uppermost node on the head is called the *crown chakra*. High energy flowing into that chakra accompanies or catalyzes *yoga*, *self-realization* or *samadhi* which is an internal state of peace and joy. If the ego fears loss of control it will try to resist upward movement of spinal energy. Yoga practice purifies body and mind which mitigates this fear. Kundalini energy can then naturally flow up the spine.

*The entire cosmos is filled with prana. During meditation a kind of static energy is built up because you are keeping your body and mind motionless, still. When the body and mind are active, the energy is discharged by all the movements. During meditation, when you stop the discharging, the prana continues to get produced. It's like charging a battery. When there's no discharge from the battery and the battery is fully charged it becomes a storage battery. During meditation, due to the prana which is static, pressure is built up and the energy rises up through the spinal column. All the stored dormant energy is released and opens up the nerve centers and rises upward. Through meditation, you become a well-charged battery.*
*– Swami Satchidananda*

# 30 ∞ KUNDALINI CAUTION ∞

Huichol String Painting - Cristobal Gonzalez

Unleashed kundalini can result in greater self-awareness and sensory perception, pre-cognition, levitation, sharpened intuition, mind reading and myriad of other capabilities. I suspect that purported miracles performed by biblical and other historical figures may have been the result of such energy surges.

Some people mistakenly practice yoga, particularly its breath control techniques in a quest for extraordinary abilities that are conferred by the increased kundalini energy. This type of motivation was considered ill-advised by Swami Satchidananda. He stressed that desire for extraordinary powers is typically born out of egotistical motivations, which can result in even greater egotism once the powers are attained.

Swami Satchidananda rarely spoke of kundalini energy. When he did so, it was to warn against practices designed to <u>force</u> energy upward along the spine. He maintained that a natural spontaneous surge is beneficial and safe. Gurudev said that this would naturally occur by detoxifying the body and calming the mind with gentle yoga practice. He noted that by exercising moderation in practicing yoga one can avoid the unpleasant side effects of too much spinal energy before the body and mind can handle it. If the electrical surge meets with resistance from mind or body impurities it can cause a short circuit and injury. The result can be illness, psychosis-like conditions or involuntary hyperactive behaviors.

My mentor was not alone in noting that spinal energy flow results in a sublime state but if forced or premature such flows may cause problems. The swami's note of caution against forcing spinal energy has an equivalent in the mystical Judaic tradition of Kabala which offers "knowledge of God". Pious Jews practice intensive non-stop meditation on kabalistic diagrams and words related to their God. The practice is restricted to very serious adherents who undertake the meditation and study with a pure heart. The result is said to end in God knowledge which I interpret to mean a samadhi experience. This practice was guarded and kept as secret for centuries. Considering the power of the energy released by the intensity of Kabala practice, the tradition of restricting its techniques to only the well prepared is a safeguard to prevent injury to the practitioner. This is analogous to the yogis maintaining that purification of body and mind is necessary before being subjected to unleashed spinal energy.

I experienced ill effects from a forced premature kundalini awakening in 1971. At that time a popular activity of my yoga brothers and sisters was to attend retreats hosted by Charles Berner who later renamed himself Yogeshwar Muni. He ran "enlightenment intensives" at his home in the Southern California desert. Most of the San Francisco IYI community and those in the Los Angeles group attended Berner events. Charles promised instant enlightenment. Many who went to his retreats came back after a few days deemed *enlightened* by Mr. Berner

At first, I resisted going to the Berner events but my friends urged me to go and "become enlightened". Later on I reluctantly agreed to do so. The program involved taking massive doses of vitamins and niacin while sitting before another participant while alternately asking and answering the inquiry, "Tell me who you are" then changing partners every 15 minutes. This went on for 15 hours a day for three days. I was the only attendee that was not declared enlightened. Instead I had a premature rush of energy in my spine that met with a blockage and this induced intense fear and physical pain in my mind and body. I experienced temporary insanity, tremors, pain and fear. Because of this, I now believe that adverse emotional or mental conditions in some people are caused by awakened kundalini energy that short-circuits when it tries to rise but is resisted by the ego. When I called Gurudev to relate my experience, he made some recommendations and then said, "Who was to say that you were not already enlightened?"

As the years passed, I continued to use Gurudev's gentle yoga methods to purify my mind and body. As a result I experienced the positive aspects of natural spinal energy without the side-effects.

## 31 ∞ EASE THE DISEASE ∞

Swami Satchidananda consistently emphasized the importance of a healthy life-style and yoga to support wellness and healing of emotional or physical illness. He often remarked, "At one time you were at ease, then you disturbed your ease and you became *dis-eased*. You can choose to restore your ease." The medical community agrees. It recognizes stress and unhealthy diet as the cause of many maladies while validating yoga as a therapy to diminish pain, stress and heart problems.

An example of the swami's approach to healing and life-style change occurred at a bookstore in Burlingame, CA where the owner cornered him and detailed particulars of her chronic physical affliction. The swami said, "If you meditate for one hour every day we will see what can be done and your condition should improve." The woman's response was, "I cannot do this because of my crowded schedule of responsibilities." Gurudev then inquired, "Do you have time to meditate for 30 minutes each day?" "Oh, Swami, my monkey-mind will not stay still for that long!" Then the swami asked, "Can you can spend 15 minutes thinking about me every day?" Her immediate response was affirmative, "I would love to do that!" As he departed, Gurudev turned to me and said, "If people get instant healing without making changes to correct the cause of the problem, their illness will just return later-on."

Gurudev once travelled to an Indian village so that he could preside over the dedication of a temple that Mr. Mahalingum restored. More than a thousand people lined the streets and many were there to solicit his healing for their afflictions.

Indian Villagers Greeting Swami Satchidananda *

After the swami made his way through the throng and arrived at the dedication site, there was only a small group that presented themselves at the ceremony out of the thousands that had lined the street. Surveying the scene, he commented, "Aha, those people wanted instant healing and boons from the swami without doing anything. They didn't come to listen about how to change their lives to eliminate the causes of illness. Even if they are healed, unless they change their ways the same problems will return."

Gurudev's ability to catalyze healing was demonstrated by how he had helped me. During one of his retreat programs it was mentioned that I was leaving to have an operation for an ulcer causing a critical condition accompanied by intense pain. My MD had prescribed a regimen of belladonna and Tums but it was not helping. The swami's advice was, "Do not go to these doctors, they will give you surgery and medicine and it will just get worse. Do this instead - eat fresh yogurt no more than 5 days old, rice, grated skin of pomegranate and cooked fenugreek seeds. Eat as much as you want whenever you want but only this until the inflammation subsides." I followed the directions for 3 weeks and then most of the pain vanished. I also lost 30 excess pounds. Six months later, my doctor confirmed that I was ulcer-free. Thanks to Gurudev's directions I avoided invasive surgery and the problem never returned. Limiting my food intake and using specific foods for healing as my mentor advised inspired me to make permanent positive changes in my eating habits. This improved my health from then on.

Gurudev's remedial and health maintenance prescriptions were a lifestyle bundle that included hatha yoga postures, breathing routines, organic vegetarian diet and a stress-free state of mind, meditation along with Indian Ayurvedic herbs, massage and folk medicine. With these simple tools he was able to help many people improve their health.

Dean Ornish, MD conducted medical trials at Baylor College and published his findings in academic journals proving that lifestyle changes reverse heart disease. The lifestyle changes that he studied were yoga teachings from Swami Satchidananda. His findings were that yoga practices not only improved the health of patients but they also *reversed* heart disease. As a result of his study and follow-up work, Dr. Ornish became more famous than Gurudev and arguably an even more effective advocate of yoga practices for health. No doubt this gratified my mentor because he often said that the public knows a good teacher by the quality of his students.

When Dean Ornish was a young medical student, the future career of this medical pioneer was boosted by the swami. I was with my teacher at a Stanford University seminar when Dean approached and mentioned that he was giving thought to discontinuing his degree program. Fortunately for the advancement of medical knowledge Dean Ornish heeded Gurudev's encouragement to continue.

The same kind of advice given to Dr. Ornish benefitted me when I was a PhD student at UC Berkeley. With the revolutionary thinking of those times and my emersion in yoga, I felt that my graduate degree program was not relevant and I wanted to quit. When I mentioned this to Gurudev, he would not hear of it. He said, "Even though you feel this way, I advise you to complete your studies. The mind should not be allowed to be so changeable." This call to discipline the mind was to be a recurring theme in the Swami's talks and in his advice to me over the years.

# 32 ∞ YOGA THERAPY ∞

Swami Satchidananda by Stephen Holland

*Stephen Madhavan Holland is a successful artist whose sport-themed canvases and posters are shown in prominent galleries. Famous teams and personalities have designated him to paint their official portrayals. He followed and personally knew Swami Satchidananda for decades. Like Stephen's paintings that capture and portray real-life scenes, he documents how Gurudev catalyzed his healing, recovery and his life.*

The year was 1987. I had been struggling on and off with heroin addiction for over 30 years. At that time I was living in Santa Barbara with a wonderful woman who was the love of my life. I should have been extremely happy but my insecurities would drive me crazy. I resumed using heroin again for over year. Then I felt fed-up. My money was running out and everything in my life was starting to fall apart. I was sick and disheartened and was it was time to stop.

I called Swami Satchidananda in Virginia and asked him if he could help me. He said that I should come out to join him at his Yogaville. I said that I would do that and that I would come right away. I told Gurudev that I had been using the drug all day every day for over a year and that I was very afraid of being sick. I asked him if he could fix it so I did not get sick. Now I know he did not like questions like that so I just packed my bags and I flew to Virginia.

When I landed at the airport the swami was overseeing a building at Yogaville. He had a few of his people to bring me to him. He greeted me and introduced me to some of his people around him. He said, "This is my dear child Madhavan. He is not feeling well and he came here to be healed. I want you all to take care of him." He looked over at me and he said, "Don't worry, you won't die and if you get sick we have a hole to throw you in but you won't get sick." He looked around smiling at everybody and said, see he wants to play but he doesn't want to pay!" Then he looked over at me and squeezed my shoulder and said, "Don't worry you'll be all right." He meant what he said because after a year of steadily using heroine I had I only had one of withdrawal symptom and that was that I couldn't sleep. I was pleasantly surprised that had no other withdrawal symptoms.

For the first three days Gurudev kept me at Yogaville and let me wander around and do whatever I pleased. After that he put me on a fast and with an intestinal cleanser. I was on the fast for one week. I could not sleep at all. Someone gave me a Walkman with some tapes of yoga chants. I just listened to the chanting over and over and over again. During this time it felt like my insides were being scrapped by a roto-rooter.

After fasting for one week I got out of bed in the morning and I said to myself, "Wow, I feel good!" It felt something like a fever had broken. So I waited until seven o'clock in the morning and I went downstairs and picked the phone and called Gurudev. I was in the habit of speaking with or seeing the swami every day that I was there. He picked up the phone and said, "So you're feeling better but you are very weak. I have been looking in on you since you came."

I was stunned when Gurudev told me that all the toxins were out of my system and that from then on I would never crave heroine because the cravings were gone. He added that I would never crave it again even if someone tied me down and injected me. He said that my body would reject it and he would always be there between me and the heroin. I told him that I was never going back on it. I wanted to go home but he wanted me to stay for a little while to gain back my strength. I said "Well I have to meet my wife at a family function and I will come back later." He sternly told me that when I came back again I would have to stay alone.

Swami Satchidananda cured my habit 23 years ago. I've been clean ever since. I never crave and he was always there in my mind if I even thought of that. My whole life changed after being cured at Yogaville. I'm still with the wonderful woman who was living with me when I had my problem. My wife gave me a chance and now I'm happier than I ever thought possible.

-Stephen Madhavan Holland

# 33 ∞ KAFFEEKLATSCH ∞

Kaffee - Club Med Style

Swami Satchidananda used to make an annual trip to appear as the keynote speaker at the conference of the *European Union of Yoga* and on one occasion I had the privilege of joining him. The event was held at the picturesque Alpine village of Zinal which was situated in the beautiful snow-peaked mountains and valleys of Switzerland. With its cow dotted green meadows and quaint architecture it was like a fairytale world.

The affable host of the conference was always Gerard Blitz, the general secretary of the Union and the founder of *Club Med*. Mr. Blitz was a well known yoga adept, author and teacher. Despite his business success and fame, he was a humble man and a great admirer of Gurudev, showing him personal attention and respect. It was evident that this was reciprocal.

Gerard Blitz and Swami Satchidananda

Mr. Blitz's yoga event provided palate pleasing upscale French and German vegetarian cuisine prepared by Club Med chefs. I was particularly fond of their morning coffee and croissants. I liked to drink the beverage without sugar. The swami was also a coffee lover and made favorable remarks about the dark dense French brew served in large bowls. The Club Med coffee was not unlike that from Madras which was a staple in Tamil Nadu Province of India where swami lived as a child.

One morning after fetching my coffee, I entered a dining area with a breathtaking view of the snow-peaked Alpine mountaintops. Gurudev was seated at the head of a long table that was full with conference attendees except for one vacant seat to his immediate right. He motioned me to sit there. Watching me as I sipped my coffee he said, "You might like it better with some sweetness." When I put my bowl down, he added a teaspoon of sugar and said, "Try it this way." When I sipped, I immediately felt elevated and peaceful.

"It is very good your way, Gurudev" I remarked. He then added another spoon of sugar and said, "Here, try this." I complied and as I sipped I started to leave my body. "This is even better." I remarked and his response was "It should always be this way." Yet a third round of sugar was dispensed by my teacher and I experienced unprecedented blissful peace and joy. The swami then turned to talk to a nearby person while I sat there transfixed. After everyone left the table my body remained seated for 15 minutes or so while I enjoyed the best meditation of my life up to that time.

Coffee with my mentor in Zinal provided ample inspiration for me to continue and intensify my yoga practice. What happened is a good example of how a master can use any situation and setting, formal or informal to transfer energy to a student and encourage him/her in yoga practice.

Swami Satchidananda in Switzerland **

## 34 ∞ **HOLIDAY MAHAL** ∞

Most visitors to India dare not drive on the highways. This is a potentially lethal game, best played by hired "professional drivers" only. Many main routes were two lane roads with no centerline and paved with peril. Everyone drove as fast as possible, weaving in and out of traffic and passing whenever they wished, irrespective of on-coming traffic. There were more commercial trucks than autos and they were all in a big hurry. The roadway was shared with throngs of pedestrians, ox carts, bikes, three wheeled "taxis" and the occasional motorbike carrying a father, a mother and a small child or two. Every now and then, it was necessary to swerve around a freshly run-over corpse lying in the middle of the road under a white sheet.

In 1977 the vehicle for most India roadway journeys was the

*Hindustani Ambassador.* This automobile was an Indian-built copy of a 1948 British Morris Oxford four door sedan. Its production ran more or less unchanged from 1958 until 2003. This postwar English engineering was not necessarily a good thing when it came to suspension, brakes, seat comfort and the absence of devises such as heaters, air conditioning and seat belts. In those days, Indians had little choice. In the 70s, the Ambassador was the only domestically produced car and therefore the only affordable one.

Tariffs on foreign-made cars were at about 100%. Gurudev's close friend, Mr. Mahalingum maintained a stable of 1956 to 1960 model autos for daily corporate use. I considered them collectors' relics due to their huge tailfins and gaudy original paint from those exuberant years. Mahalingum was not a collector but felt the need to avoid the tariff expenses from importing new foreign cars. Although his cars looked old they were fitted with brand new Mercedes engines and running gear.

Part of the Mahalingum Fleet *

Agra was the destination of one hair-raising motor tour with

Gurudev. When he alighted at the destination, greeting him was the renowned jazz flutist, Paul Horn who ushered our party into the Taj Mahal where he regaled the swami with a flute concert that he was recording. The 60 by 80 foot solid white marble dome resonated with the peaceful notes. Echoes and overtones became part of the innovative ethereal music. Paul neglected to apply for permission to record in the venerable structure and was asked to leave but he disregarded instructions and played for Gurudev anyway. Eventually the head guard seemed moved by the unexpected scene on his beat and instead of throwing everyone out he allowed the session to continue. I wondered to myself if Gurudev's appearance had anything to do with Paul's reprieve. The recording was issued commercially and sold over a million copies under the title *Inside the Taj Mahal.*

The day spent at Agra was also significant for more reasons than the visit to the Taj. After listening to Paul Horn, our party proceeded to the nearby Holiday Inn to take lunch. Seeing the familiar American hotel sign near this iconic Indian location seemed surrealistic. The hotel was a clone of those in the U.S. except for the fragrant open sewage disposal pond behind the complex.

Holiday Inn, Agra India

Lunch was served in a night club room where the other clients were a group of burly beer drinking Russian-Soviet civil engineers glaring suspiciously at our party. A live combo was playing and my teacher approached and spoke to the band leader. He then signaled me to replace the drummer. I was once a semi-professional percussionist but was years out of practice. As I sat down at the drums the band began playing *California Here I Come*. This energized the Soviet diners who were inebriated by that time. They clapped and attempted to sing along in Russian. This was a welcome change from the suspicion-tainted attitude that they projected earlier. Perhaps this was a hint of the Glasnost to come in later years.

After lunch, we went to a replica of *Deer Park*. Swamiji sat under a bhodhi tree and gave a satsang (spiritual talk) about the life and teachings of Buddha. Buddhist monks who were passing-by heard the discourse, sat down to listen and several took photos. It was an interfaith event. These Buddhists were hearing about their prophet from a teacher of Hindu origin.

# 35 ∞ DIVINE DANCE ∞

Lord of Dance Nataraja - Favorite Deity of Swami Satchidananda

During my trip to India with Gurudev, he visited his boyhood home in the province of Tamil Nadu. When the provincial governor learned that the swami and his party were nearby he insisted that we attend his ball as guests of honor. It was held at the governor's residence, built in the bygone days of the British Raj complete with beautiful English gardens. The mansion was filled with important politicians and public figures dressed in formal eveningwear. As we entered the Governor personally introduced his dinner guests to Gurudev. Gourmet food was then presented on silver platters by attentive white-gloved uniformed servants with silver tongs served on fine English china imprinted with the governor's crest. A large orchestra entered the hall as the Governor announced that the band had rehearsed some modern American tunes in honor of the swami and his American students. For the second time on the India trip we graciously endured a rousing performance of *California Here I Come*, followed by a delightful mix of American dance standards.

My teacher paired up the male and female members of his entourage which included monks and nuns and asked them to dance together. The Governor then introduced a female member of his family to Gurudev. At the governor's behest, the swami and the woman then danced American style to slow music and rocked to an up-tempo ditty. Attired in his long orange robe, beard and sandals Gurudev was a better dancer than anyone else on the floor.

# 36 ∞ MOUNA SWAMI'S ISLAND ∞

Island in the Ganges River near Rishikesh *

The reception that Gurudev and his party received on a tiny island in the middle of the Ganges River near Rishikesh contrasted with the lavish soiree at the Governor's Mansion. On the island we were received in total silence.

We alighted from a large row boat to find one human inhabitant of the island and he did not speak to us. His voice was not impaired but for years he had chosen never to speak to anyone. He was called Mouna (silent) Swami. We brought offerings to our "host" consisting of a mixture of grains and hay. Mouna Swami received and distributed them to his permanent freeloading tenants – his cow herd. We then sat on hay bales facing Mouna Swami. As others were meditating I was wondering why we had come to this bovine sanctuary but then I felt a great peace. When we left, Mouna Swami remained in silence, alone with his cows. Back on the boat I thought, "On that island, the sound of silence was always herd."

# 37 ∞ AIRBORNE AVATAR ∞

Swami Satchidananda loved to fly. He took lessons to become a pilot but never obtained a license. This was because with his Indian accent, airport flight controllers had a hard time clearly communicating with him over the radio. Some of Gurudev's students were pilots with access to planes and he never had trouble commandeering their aircraft. During the final decade of his life, the swami was given a small private plane named *The Spirit of Yogaville* which he used in Virginia with the assistance of one of his students who was a licensed pilot.

The swami was a fearless flyer. Once on the way from Santa Barbara to Santa Monica, Gurudev flew the plane over restricted airspace of the naval base at Port Hueneme. Within minutes a navy warplane was right beside our wing tip. The navy pilot did a double take when he saw an elderly man in orange with long hair and a beard at the controls. His plane was so close to our aircraft that we could see his hand gestures that motioned the swami away from the air space.

Soon after being evicted from restricted airspace we flew over the mountains ringing the Simi Valley and at that point the engine started sputtering. The licensed pilot seated next to his flying guru explained that the engine was chocking on the smog from Los Angeles. He changed the carburetor mixture to compensate for low oxygen content. Although there was no control panel on my body to adjust for bad air, I remembered that yogic breathing can regulate oxygen content so I urgently practiced pranayama to compensate.

The balance of the flight to Santa Monica and our later return was uneventful until we passed by Ventura. Flying over the blue Pacific with Gurudev still at the controls he took the craft down to about 20 feet over the water as ocean spray splashed the windshield. All of a sudden he put the plane in a steep climb, leaving my stomach at sea level. As soon as we gained altitude, a severe downdraft lowered the altitude of the craft almost to the crest of the waves. If Gurudev did not have the intuition to gain altitude when he did, our plane ride would have transformed into a submarine excursion! Once my head was out of the clouds and my feet were well supported by good old Mother Earth I wondered about taking additional airborne excursions with my beloved mentor. I never answered this question but thereafter I found myself happily airborne with my guru many more times.

## 38 ∞ THE INVISIBLE MAN ∞

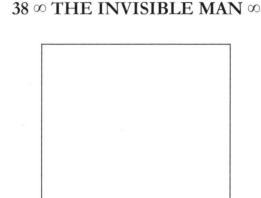

Portrait of Invisible Man by Eyenoe Seaum

Swami Satchidananda was a striking tall figure with a long beard and hair, attired in orange robes and radiating a beatific countenance. Passers-by invariably took notice and their gaze would follow him as he walked by. Gurudev seemed to encourage this recognition as a kind of PR to publicize yoga. People who did not know him would smile, wave or approach him and start a conversation. Children were particularly attracted to the swami and he always reciprocated their interest with mirth and frolic.

I knew my teacher's public persona to be consistent except on one occasion at the Santa Barbara Downtown Mall. Gurudev always enjoyed playing with electronic gadgets and exploring the latest technologies. While he was window shopping at the mall, a yoga student approached and reported that the swami's friend was having a sudden health crisis. Gurudev immediately left the store and turned up the slight collar on his over-garment. We proceeded through the mall toward the parking garage to drive to the aid of the stricken person. As we made our way through the densely packed Saturday shopping crowd not one person noticed, nodded, smiled, waved or otherwise greeted him. As a result of his will and intent, people could not see or approach the swami to impede his progress. I thought to myself, "So, those sci-fi movies about invisible men were true!"

I had read that yogis in India were said to have exceptional powers called *siddhis* that included the ability to become invisible. Now I realized that becoming invisible does not have to do with a potion or physical process as seen in the movies. It is an internal mindset that controls the yogi's public persona. In the movies, a person made invisible would physically disappear but in the real world becoming invisible does not involve disappearance. It is generated by withdrawing controlling or redirecting one's energy so that others do not notice the human being right in front of their eyes.

The shopping center experience with the swami led me to understand that the power to not be seen by others is the opposite of the ability to attract people or their attention. This opposite power is known as *charisma*. This chain of thought led me to a hypothesis: invisibility and charisma are in a sense both siddhis. Yoga adepts and other high energy people can have either or both abilities by regulating their inner thoughts and energies. Gurudev had the ability to withdraw his energy from the public space and the converse also was true. In most other situations it suited his purposes to be seen and project his presence in public settings.

In India one sees many sidewalk exhibitions of extraordinary abilities such as mind reading, predicting the future or levitating. Some are easily acquired simply by using yogic breathing techniques. On the street in India such abilities are often displayed to get money or attract followers. In this regard, Gurudev mentioned to me that Swami Nityananda (who was Baba Muktananda's guru) rose to prominence by lying at roadside near the entrance to a race track and correctly advising people who passed by which horse to bet on and it would always be the winner of the days big race.

Gurudev taught that exceptional powers or siddhis were a by-product of yogic practice but developing them was not to be considered a desirable goal. There are four good reasons for not seeking such powers: they can make a person egotistical, there is a danger that they can be misused for selfish purposes, the energy that is built-up to accomplish willful acts and selfish uses of the powers can impact mind or body in a disruptive fashion, and the exercise of powers can be a diversion from working toward the goal of yoga. These pitfalls can be obstacles to the self-fulfillment, peace and joy that yoga delivers when correctly practiced. I realized that my teacher had an extensive array of extraordinary powers such as the ability to become invisible but he only exercised them in subtle, barely noticeable ways and even then only to help other people.

## 39 ∞ WIZARD OF OM ∞

Swami Satchidananda loved watching magic shows and he even had a few tricks up his sleeve. He looked like a wizard and I knew he actually was one after he manifested positive events in my life and even predicted a tragedy.

I loved living in Santa Barbara. Swami Satchidananda asked me to relocate there to help incubate a yoga community. To my mind it was the best city in the entire world. Winter temperatures averaged 68 degrees while summers were a comfortable 73. Pristine beaches were never crowded and the hills were ornamented with Spanish architecture, palm trees, avocado and tropical fruit orchards. I planned to spend my whole life there and never wanted to move.

After a few years when the Santa Barbara yoga community relocated to Virginia I was faced with a hard choice. Gurudev advised that it was in my best interest to move there but I resisted and decided to stay in California. Just six months later, I was unexpectedly unemployed when the consulting company where I was a senior executive was sold. Then Gurudev once more advised me that the best thing I could do was leave California and stay for a while at his *Satchidananda Ashram – Yogaville* that was relocated in Virginia. This time I finally followed his suggestion but after six months there, bored and restless I decided to investigate the possibility of a part-time teaching position.

The first public college built in the US was the prestigious University of Virginia which was only one hour away from Yogaville. It was originally conceived of and built by Thomas Jefferson. When I arrived there, I walked unannounced into the Department Chairman's office without an appointment. I introduced myself, presented my resume and inquired about a teaching position. The chairman said, "This is curious, the professor who taught the classes that you are qualified for just resigned a few days ago. The fall semester is upon us and here you are. The position is yours!" After that semester, I was appointed as a full-time tenure track Associate Professor. I had harbored a dream to teach at a major university ever since I was a graduate student. It was fulfilled by simply following my teacher's advice to move closer to him in Virginia.

Another extraordinary power that Gurudev possessed was very strong intuition. One day after I moved to Virginia he called me aside and asserted, "You should sell your property in California. There are earthquakes and fires and one never knows what will happen".

My mentor often warned against being attached to anything. Unfortunately I was attached to what I called my Santa Barbara Ranch. I purchased 11 of the original 62 acres that had been

Yogaville West before my teacher ordered it to be sold. My property consisted of a 100 year old farmhouse and barn situated on a creek with oak and citrus trees together with an avocado orchard. The property was quickly gaining in value. My brother and his family lived there and I wanted to keep it for them beyond my lifetime. Two other sets of tenants also lived at the ranch.

After a few years, my brother and other tenants suddenly moved away. The only remaining couple was excited about their planned move to Hawaii but tragically they were still on the ranch when it was hit by the Painted Cave Fire and the wife perished. Flames 100 feet high raced at 60 miles per hour down the hills and burned several thousand acres. Hundreds of homes were lost including my farmhouse and barn which was filled with antique furniture, family keepsakes and my racing boat with trophies. Also lost were a newly purchased motor home and an uninsured antique car collection. For me, this event was certainly a real-world lesson in the swami's teachings about the need for non-attachment! Had I taken the swami's advice to sell, I could have avoided such a tragedy.

I reflected that my ranch which was the site of death and destruction was formerly part of the Yogaville property. I shuddered to contemplate what would have befallen our yoga community if our teacher had not the foresight of a wizard to relocate!

## 40 ∞ MY IYI HIGH ∞

During the decades that I was privileged to spend time with Swami Satchidananda I often experienced a blissful samadhi-like state so natural and familiar that I took it for granted. If I would have tried to put my feelings into words they would have been something like, "Ahhh, this is the real me! I am, was and always will be this way." The feeling proved to be ephemeral when the peaceful experience of a timeless state *seemed* to evaporate as my every-day mundane thoughts and worries returned and infiltrated my joyous and tranquil mind.

Gurudev confirmed the difficulty of maintaining a tranquil mind while we were visiting a sacred cave located in the Indian Himalayas adjacent to Rishikesh. Although the cave was situated under a busy road on a mountainside, it was quieter than any other place that could be imagined. I recognized that inhabiting this venue for weeks or months such as he did could have a profound positive or negative effect on anyone. It was said that he attained permanent self-realization at this cave. While revisiting there Gurudev said to me, "It is easy to be a yogi in a cave – but can the yogi be peaceful in the world?" I interpreted his words to mean: "It is easier to experience yourself as the essence of peace and joy in meditation and through other yogic practices but retaining such a state when participating in everyday life is much harder to do."

The closer I observed my mentor the more it was apparent to me that he was in a perpetual state of joy and peace no matter what he was doing. From time to time I experienced snippets of what Gurudev enjoyed but they always seemed to evaporate. Why did his sublime state persist while mine vanished? The answer that came was that my teacher's mind did not regress to a pattern of desire and anxiety as mine had a tendency to do. I realized that the Calm Lake allegory used by my teacher in his talks was a description of his state of mind and why it never changed.

A tale told by Leela Marcum who is an accomplished artist and yogi casts a humorous light on the relationship between the experience of bliss and the need to ignore the vagaries of the mind. She recounts:

In the very beginning of 1974, Gurudev came to visit me and my parents in Los Alamos, NM. Ish and Brahmi Cowan came along on the trip. It was their honeymoon. When visitors came, we always took them to all the wonderful sites that we enjoyed. Although it was January in the mountains and snow was everywhere, I just had a bee in my bonnet that Gurudev, Ish and Brahmi had to see the caldera of Valle Grande in the Jemez. It was a mountain road, not plowed. At one point, it started to snow and the snow got so deep that the road got treacherous. We had to stop and put chains on the car. Rather, my dad put chains on the car. It wasn't an easy task in the middle of all the deepening snow. My parents were not happy that I had insisted taking this trip and were anxious about the uncertainty of getting home safely. I was quite confident that everything would be just fine. Gurudev, Brahmi, and Ish were taking it in stride, or so it seemed, at least. It irritated my mother that we seemed so oblivious to the dangers of the road. While we were standing around watching and trying to be encouraging, since there wasn't much else we could do to help, my mother said, "I understand that ignorance is bliss and I can see that you are all blissful!" Gurudev loved it and roared with laughter. He told that story in public many times since then."

I think that the swami often retold Leela's story to underscore her mother's recognition of our bliss in her sarcastic way and whether she consciously knew it or not added the important perspective that a good way to become blissful is to practice ignorance of self-centered concerns.

Part of the value of the teachings of Swami Satchidananda is to support people in promoting bliss in a peaceful mind that comes from an ability to disregard (aka "be ignorant of") the phantom monsters of desire and anxiety created by a self absorbed ego-centered mind. The teachings promoting this are to be found in the swami's Integral Yoga®.

Living in today's high pressure artificial and money driven environment it is easy to forget the value of a permanently peaceful and joy drenched existence. Yet, some people who have been badly burned by the modern lifestyle, long for it. These days it is difficult to cloister oneself in a cave until a self-realization experience dawns and even more difficult to maintain a semblance of peace and joy when and if it manifests. Swami Satchidananda had some good answers to addressing such dilemmas. He is no longer available in person but fortunately, he showed great foresight in leaving behind a treasure trove of videos, books, CDs and class training instructions to supplant the need for meditation caves and eliminate the quandary of attaining and then losing track of a sense of joy and peace. His teachings are available on-line, on YouTube and in videos of the swami's talks, classes, retreats and publications offered by the Integral Yoga Institute –the IYI and its mother organization, Satchidanda Ashram-Yogaville.

*"Knowledge-bliss, knowledge - bliss, bliss absolute: In all conditions I am knowledge-bliss absolute. I'm not the body, not the mind, immortal self I am!"*
*-HH Sri Swami Sivananda*

## 41 ∞ CUPID & SWAMI ∞

Although Swami Satchidananda was a monk he did not recommend monastic paths for most people. He valued the mutual commitment between two people who join together to serve each other, their children and the community at large. He emphasized that there should be a strong selfless service flavor to a marriage or partnership. He viewed relationships as opportunities to practice karma yoga by always putting the other person first. He explained that conflicts between partners can be beneficial egodectomies that challenge each one to recognize and reduce selfishness. This kind of dynamic is helpful for progress in yoga. Unselfish love and devotion in a long-term relationship is yoga. They function as bhakti or the path of devotion. The swami strongly cautioned against what he called "business" in a relationship, which meant giving to the partner but expecting to get something back in-kind.

Before Swami Satchidananda migrated to the US he had been raised and immersed in traditional Indian culture that tightly restricted sexual behavior. Unwed sex was taboo as was any display of the female form. Women of upper Indian castes were expected to be chaste until marriage

On a trip to India in 1977, a tour group with Gurudev underscored the difference between Indian and Western attitudes toward the human form. When our party went to the beach, my fair-haired former wife donned a modest American-style bathing suit. This contrasted with garb worn by the dark skinned Indian females on the beach and in the water. They were wearing saris that covered their entire bodies from shoulder to foot. My wife was immediately surrounded by two dozen Indian men standing around gawking and speechless. They had never seen a woman in swimwear in their entire lives.

Given his Indian background, cultural shock must have been intense for Swami Satchidananda when he arrived in 1960s America in the midst of radical young female hippies who wore scanty clothing and flaunted their bodies, engaging in sensual dancing and sexual promiscuity. As coed housing and communities formed around my teacher, sexual high-jinks continued the same as before he came on the scene. Gurudev accepted and tolerated such American sexual norms in his groups. Our Los Angeles institute had a huge swanky mansion with a swimming pool in the Hollywood Hills. One evening Gurudev arrived there to give a talk but instead all of his time was consumed by complaints and concerns of the house members about bruised feelings in the prevailing atmosphere of rampant sexual behavior and betrayals. Our teacher's immediate response was to impose a ban on sex outside of marriage for his entire organization. He reminded the residents that if their thoughts were disturbed by being occupied with sexual desire and betrayal, very little progress could be made in calming the mind to reap the benefits of yoga.

On several occasions the swami mentioned that sex was a normal part of a married couple's life and called it fun that they can have. He preached sexual moderation even in monogamous relationships. His teachings were consistent with traditional yogic thought. Control of the mind and its desires was part of yoga practice and he deemed moderation in all things as desirable. Yoga texts and my mentor advised against dissipating too much energy or prana through sexual excessive actitivity.

The change of policy on sexual behavior at Gurudev's yoga institutes was one reason for the decision of the two top executives and others at the Los Angeles institute to switch paths and join with a Buddhist teacher who permitted, indulged in and encouraged indiscriminant sex, drugs and alcohol. One of these former executives rose to the top of that organization but ironically passed away from a sexual disease when he was about 40 years old shortly after his Buddhist teacher passed away from alcoholism at the age of

47.

For some, the sensible limitations on sexuality and partner relations in Gurudev's closely knit yoga communities brought with them an enhanced and welcomed sense of stability and tranquility. For those who took the established norms seriously there was one less distraction from yogic practice and lifestyle.

Human desires are not easily banished by edict and over the years Integral Yoga experienced its share of muted gossip, scandals and misbehavior as one might expect from a certain proportion of members in any community. Some of those who could not abide by established norms in the group including myself sought Gurudev's advice on the matter. He would say, "Even though you are not living up to all of this, you know the ideal; be discrete, stay here and do the best that you can to work towards the goal." To others that felt compelled to be wilder and more overt he would say, "Go with my blessings, do what you wish and come back if and when you get it out of your system and you are ready."

The last word I heard directly from my teacher about sexual relationships in a community came when he was watching a TV news program about Rajaneesh who had been a teacher in a community that he established in Oregon. The news report told of open orgies and drug taking resulting in negative health issues. The community had been closed down with Rajaneesh deported and his lieutenant jailed. Gurudev quipped ironically, "Maybe Rajaneesh had the right idea – let them get it out of their systems and after that they can get down to serious practice." I interpreted his remark to be about the difficulty of stabilizing young sexually active Americans who have previously been exposed to a patently sexual culture.

*Please don't do business in the name of love. The hubby looks at the wife and says, 'Honey, I love you,' and then keeps on looking at her expecting her to turn around and say, 'Darling, I love you too.' And, if that fails or she even hesitates to return that love, where will the honey go? Straight to the divorce lawyer. That means, "I love you, but only if you love me. If you don't give your love, I won't love you anymore." That's not love but it is business. There is unhappiness in relationships, because we do business constantly. Let's not mistake business for love. Love for the joy of loving and you'll always enjoy.*

  *–Swami Satchidananda*

# 42 ∞ DOWN TO EARTH GURU ∞

Gurudev Sailing in the Santa Barbara Channel  *

Swami Satchidananda was a very good example of the benefits of yoga. Well into his late sixties I saw him demonstrate difficult hatha yoga postures even though he no longer practiced them. When he was in his seventies he startled me when he stepped out of the car while I was slowly driving toward the entrance of his driveway that ran over a very steep hill to his La Paz home in Santa Barbara. He ran up the slope along side of the driveway and was at the top sooner than the car finished its climb. When I arrived after him, he exclaimed, "So you thought the old swami was frail and helpless!"

There was no question that Gurudev always was a very good example of yogic lifestyle. Until he passed away in his late-eighties, he exhibited no memory loss or mental lapses. He also retained his youthful vitality, and keen mind that was quick with advice, stories, puns and other jokes. The Swami knew better than anyone how to enjoy himself, how best to entertain others and especially how to be childlike and playful with youngsters.

Swami Satchidanda and Students in Sri Lanka    *

The left and right sides of Gurudev's brain seemed to be well balanced, intuitive and intellectually profound. He understood mechanics, repaired cars, built model planes and could explain how most machines work. He kept up with current events all the time and consumed a large amount of media content daily, often referring to news items as examples in his public talks. I was 28 years younger than my mentor and during public events, travel and social interaction he possessed far more physical and mental stamina than I did.

When I was fortunate to spend day after day with Gurudev, I recognized another factor that kept his health radiant and his body and mind energized. In addition to being an embodiment of yoga he maintained a very well regulated daily life and routine. When possible he would wake up, eat, sleep and conduct his routines almost to the same exact hour and minute every day as though each activity was mechanically regulated.  Every day he would nap after lunch. I started to imitate the swami's routine and found that a regular schedule kept my mind and body in optimal condition.

My mentor had great self-discipline in every aspect of his life but he was by no means an ascetic dour-faced wimp in a turban with a diaper on a mountaintop. Even though he advised his students to be careful about caffeine, coffee was a daily treat that he enjoyed along with Pepperidge Farm cookies. In later years his doctor advised against caffeinated coffee and butter. Those around him tried to enforce this restriction but when outside his home and his attendants backs were turned, he took great delight in mischievously prompting one of us to sneak him the banned treats.

Gurudev was very fond of pizza which created additional endearment on the part of his students when they went with him to local pizza parlors. Sometimes he acted as host. He had a favorite parlor on both coasts. During his Santa Barbara years I took him to his favorite place for pizza every week. On my 40th birthday Gurudev asked me to take him out for pizza but he had secretly arranged a surprise birthday party at our favorite place.

Even though his assistants usually cooked for him I knew Gurudev to be a good cook himself. Most of the recipes that his helpers used were based upon instructions that he gave them. His one regular sized meal was eaten at mid-day and was usually an Indian curry dish or a cucumber sandwich. At home, he sat on the floor and ate in traditional South Indian fashion using only his right hand without fork or spoon.

Gurudev summoned me to Malibu on one Sunday. He was staying there as a guest at Carol King's rented beachfront home. Carol was away for the day. As soon as I walked inside, Gurudev commanded me to sit down. He then went to the stove and dished out a steaming bowl of the Indian dish known as *upma* which he had just finished preparing. It was his recipe and one of the best meals I ever consumed. After he and I ate, he bid me farewell.

I think that his reason for inviting me to Malibu was two-fold. First, Gurudev was alone and cooking for himself. It was not in his nature to act only on his behalf even when cooking a meal. Being a karma yogi he had the desire to share the product of his labors with someone. He knew that I was available and loved to eat. At the same time, Gurudev was showing me an example of karma yoga. On a more esoteric level, my guru was passing some of his *prana* to one of his students through the medium of *prasad*. It was traditional at the conclusion of all of Gurudev's talks that he would bless and energize a treat called *prasad* which was given to all persons present. Receiving personalized prasad in the form of upma from him had a powerful elevating effect.

Gurudev watched a considerable amount of television news programs and enjoyed movies. Every time a new James Bond movie came out he would be seen at a theatre along with a cadre of his students.

The wisdom of my mentor was great yet he had natural cultural biases. Belying his upper-middle class Indian upbringing, when I ordered an oatmeal bowl, he quipped that such food was only suitable for horses. Other dishes scorned by Gurudev included mushrooms and eggplant. His cultural biases also manifested in architectural preference. The popularity of California adobe style homes was a complete mystery to the swami because in India only poor people had homes made out of adobe which they put together with dried mud, straw, clay and handmade tiled roofs.

Gurudev was widely known and appreciated by his followers, the media and the public but there were exceptions. Some who felt that only their religion was valid did not appreciate his viewpoint. Others expected absolute perfection of a teacher and were intolerant of any human shortcomings. Teachers who become examples and icons like Swami Satchidananda are never without imperfections. Their public exposure attracts close scrutiny which makes inevitable flaws more apparent and more prone to criticism. Even so, Swami Satchidananda never hesitated to be himself. He was not afraid to show his basic human qualities.

Unlike some other teachers that I encountered, Gurudev did not try to act out an idealized concept of how a guru is supposed to act. He freely expressed displeasure, anger, impatience and other human emotions. He admitted when he was wrong. He appreciated nature, tasty food, attractive females and he enjoyed communicating with children on their own terms.

Some people were critical of Gurudev's natural human shortcomings but I thought that his imperfections made him more real and likeable. Those who expected external perfection misunderstood the nature of masters and scriptures written about them. There never was a master who escaped criticism for displaying human traits.

# 43 ∞ LOOKING BACK ∞

Swami Satchidananda at Ish Cowan's Surprise 40th Birthday Party

After Swami Satchidananda became my guru, I realized that although yoga seemed so exotic and foreign at first, his teachings were actually common sense advice with no mystery attached to them. What he taught was straight forward and simple. The only hard part was to listen carefully, understand and have the will to act upon what he patiently advised over and over again in plain English.

For years I heard from my Gurudev about what to practice and how to apply yoga. Even so, it took a long time to comprehend the meaning of his words about how life works and how to bring it all together.

Although the formula that my mentor taught is universal and found in many historic yoga texts and religious scriptures, without his personality, simple explanations, example as a role model and supercharged encouragement I could not have persisted and prevailed by merely reading books and trying to practice on my own. I haven't reached the goal but the path is now very clear. For me, it is no longer a mystery about how to find and approach the calm lake of constant peace and joy that I think is the highest prize in life.

I am very thankful for my good fortune to have spent so much time with my teacher. Even so, serving this great master was not always a bed of roses. Much of my time with him was spent as a domestic servant and it was wise for me to keep my comments to myself and my preferences abandoned. I was constantly on-call whenever I was not working at my paid employment elsewhere. Everything that I did wrong was magnified like being under a microscope. Because I was usually with the teacher, I had to sacrifice the opportunity to spend the time to culture close friendships with other members of my community. I considered these drawbacks to be a small price to pay for my experiences with Gurudev.

Gurudev and I spent a lot of time together; we shared common interests and enjoyed the company of one other. He certainly was a good friend to me. Some members of our community also considered me to be a friend of our teacher but it had never entered my mind to presume to call myself a friend of his. That was for him to decide. I believed in what he did and I simply was there to help him. My love for him was like a son feels for a father. When I accompanied him in public I acted as a bodyguard without being asked and felt prepared to sacrifice my life to protect him. In return I felt his profound love and caring. It touched me when he told others "take care of my baby boy".

Swami Satchidananda was family to me. Because he allowed me to be a constant presence in his private life for many years, I feel that I came to understand his tastes, thoughts and concerns as a family member might. Behind his exotic public persona I saw that he was in many ways a real person with typical American tastes. He liked to eat out, watch TV, make puns and corny jokes, go to the cinema, take a nap every day, drink coffee, play with electronic gadgets, talk politics, enjoy his cars, engage in hobbies and keep a regular dining and sleeping schedule. He was always ready to be of service to others and like anyone else he treasured and needed some privacy and time to relax.

The swami genuinely loved and cared for everyone in his life. He always gave back more than he received. I felt like a prince in his presence even when performing a servant's task.

Once when asked to explain why it was that I spent so much time and had direct access to Gurudev. I answered that there was a magical chemistry between us from the very first time that I met him. My next response was that he and I seemed to have many of the same interests and hobbies. There were a number of other reasons why I had the opportunity to spend so much time with my teacher. First, I had a flexible work schedule with a lot of free time in my job. Second, I had enough money to travel with and occasionally host him. Third, I was older and therefore more emotionally mature than many of his other students. Fourth, I knew business, law, finance and how to get things done in the workaday world and these capabilities were helpful to him in overseeing his institutions. Fifth, like most of his other students, I always put his interests before my own and treated him with great respect.

I recognized and appreciated my teacher's saintly aspect and celebrated his private mundane human side and short-comings as well. Because I did not harbor a pre-conceived notion of how a "guru" is supposed to be, I did not judge him. When he and I were in relaxation mode I took care to never become inappropriately casual and familiar. I recognized, respected and tried to act consistent with my teacher's roles that constantly changed according to different situations. I figured that because he gave me unconditional acceptance no matter what my state of mind, to return the favor was the least that I could do.

Swami Satchidananda believed that love should be unconditional otherwise it was "business" – giving love to get love. The love for my teacher grew to be unconditional and started extending to everyone that I knew – even myself. Because of his guidance I learned to love and treat myself and others like I treated Gurudev and he treated me. He encouraged and gave me tastes of what it feels like to visit and dwell on the banks of my inner Calm Lake. Now I can go there anytime no matter what I am doing or where I am. Many people have had similar positive experiences with this great master.

Now that my mentor has left this earth, I rarely miss him. Even though he departed, the teachings and spirit of Swami Satchidananda remains.

If you realize the peace within you and know that you are peace personified, then peace is always in you. Whenever you see that your peace is disturbed, you will immediately realize that it's disturbed because YOU disturbed it. You will realize, "Oh, I see. I threw a desire in the quiet calm lake of my mind. I wanted something, so that want fell into my calm mind, as a stone falling into a lake, and it started creating ripples." If you hadn't thrown that stone in the lake, you wouldn't have seen the ripples. The lake would always be calm and clear.

– Swami Satchidananda

THE END

# APPENDIX:
# WORDS & IMAGES

## Swami Satchidananda's Selected Sayings

Happiness is God. What kind of happiness? Eternal happiness - not temporary happiness. Temporary happiness can be found by gaining a good life partner, a few million dollars or landing a good job. But those are temporary types of happiness, is it not? No one is always happy with their partner or their job. Once you have found permanent happiness, it never goes away. And when you have it you have found God, you are in God.

When you do an act, if you have a personal motive behind it or if you expect a reward by that action, even before you start doing it, you build up tension. There is an expectation, there is anxiety. There is fear of losing something also. So you spoil the mind with which you are doing the action. Then the action itself is spoiled.

*

We don't ever lose our ease totally because ease can never be lost. It's the same case with peace. Anything that's positive is always positive. Nobody has ever created anything or destroyed anything. As such, we can never destroy ease or peace. That's the reason we call an illness a "disease." It's really just disturbed ease. If we can find out the cause of the disturbance and remove it, the ease and peace that was disturbed will return to the normal level. Any mechanism that goes out of alignment cannot function well. So simply tighten the screws and put back its alignment. That's the purpose behind all the Yoga practices.

*

The purpose of your Yoga practice is so that you can physically be easeful, mentally peaceful and socially useful. But, before you can become really useful, be peaceful. How? Prepare yourself. Self-reformation. Doctors know about this. Before they begin to operate, however urgent the operation, they take time to scrub and prepare for a sterile environment. Every one of us is an instrument. We are performing operations in this life. When will we become fit? Only when we sterilize ourselves. That's what Yoga does: It cleans the body and mind. When we have that clean body and mind, we will be good instruments and God, or the humanity, will make good use of us. And that's Yoga.

If you know certain products are produced by harming animals, you should avoid them. Of course, whatever you do, you have to cause a little pain. You kill many living beings just by breathing. Even by eating plant food, you have to kill the plants; but not completely. You just take one part of the plant, and plant the other part and that part comes forth as a new plant. So, reduce your violence and the amount of pain you cause. This is why we advocate a vegetarian diet, because animals, more than plant life, feel the pain when we kill them. Therefore, if you want to live without causing much pain, consider all these points. As long as there are nuts, beans, seeds and plants available, don't think of hunting animals. AHIMSA, nonviolence, is good for your body, mind and for your heart.

*

Cleaning the mind is very important. The mind was all clean in the beginning. We were fine originally, but we didn't want to live as fine people. We were fine but weren't satisfied with that kind of happiness, so we wanted to de-fine ourselves. Each and every one of us has a definition. I have de-fined myself as 'so-and-so.' Who are the refined people? The ones who don't have any define-ment or limitations—they don't de-fine or limit themselves in any way. We split ourselves in many ways. That means each limitation is a definement and makes us lose our fineness. To live truly as fine people means to raise above all these definements. We don't have to discard everything—we can use definitions for convenience or for fun, but don't identify with them.

*

We all have the same purpose; whatever road we take, whatever approach we take, we seem to be going toward the same goal. We all want to be happy. Not only the human being, even the animate and inanimate, animals, plants, everything and everybody wants to be happy. We have one common goal, but many ways to approach it. That's why, even in the name of religion or spirituality, we have so many approaches, according to the taste of different individuals. Let us accept all the different paths to the truth and not feel that our own approach is superior or another's is inferior. We are all walking toward the same goal: to find permanent happiness, permanent peace.

The secret of life is simple. Play your part well but don't identify with it. Remember who you are. You have a role to play in life. Act well but do not forget that you are acting. If you forget the spiritual side and think that you are a completely worldly person, there's danger that you'll be lost in illusion. If you think that you are completely spiritual and forget the world, then there is danger that people will say you are crazy. Be in the world but not of the world.

Peace and joy is the goal of every human being. Unfortunately, we think that by gathering more and more money, name and fame, we can be permanently happy. Every time we acquire something new, we feel that happiness momentarily, but we forget that this momentary joy came only after a lot of anxiety and pain, acquiring things we wanted. As soon as we get these things and feel happiness but soon the fear of losing those things comes in. This sort of restlessness continues on and on. When you stop running after things and become the master of your possessions rather than the slave, you'll live in the world as a liberated person, floating freely like a boat in the water.

We all have the same purpose; whatever road we take, whatever approach we take, we seem to be going toward the same goal. We all want to be happy. Not only the human being, even the animate and inanimate, animals, plants, everything and everybody wants to be happy. Put a plant indoors, it will slowly try to creep to the window because it wants to be happy. We have one common goal, but many ways to approach it. And that's why, even in the name of religion or spirituality, we have so many approaches, according to the taste of the individual. Let us learn to accept all the different paths to the truth and not feel that our own approach is superior or another's is inferior. We are all walking toward the same goal: to find permanent happiness, permanent peace.

*

The purpose of Yoga is to calm waves in the mind. Keep the mind still. Then, you will see your True Self in the still water of the peaceful mind. Look in a bowl of water that has waves upon its surface. Can you see your face clearly? No. If you stop all the waves, you can see your face clearly. But what should you do to stop the waves? What should you do? Don't touch the water. Don't shake it. The water becomes still by itself

– Swami Satchidananda

# ABOUT THE AUTHOR

Errol Ishwara Cowan has been a practitioner and student of yoga for 45 years. He received his mantra initiation and the name *Ishwara* from Swami Satchidananda in 1970. Three years later he started serving as a yoga teacher/lecturer, administrator and Integral Yoga Minister for the following twenty years. During that time, he served in the administration of Integral Yoga Institutes in California, assisted in the establishment of two Institute branches, three Yogaville-Satchidananda Ashram communities and was appointed the first president of the Yogaville Council in Buckingham, Virginia where Cowan co-developed the Lotus Inn and served as president of Integral Health, Inc.

Dr. Cowan holds a PhD and a MBA from the University of California at Berkeley and served as an Associate Professor of Business Administration at two California State Universities. He was also Associate Professor of Urban and Environmental Planning at the University of Virginia.

Errol founded and was CEO of Doe Bay Village Retreat on Orcas Island, WA and Hidden Valley Ranch & Retreat in Santa Barbara, CA. He was the first developer of Lake Reynovia in Virginia, co-developed Madera in Gainesville, FL and was master developer of the HOME community in Sequim, WA.

The author has been an expert witness in courts as well as a consultant to many public and private entities including Fannie Mae, the Cities of Santa Fe, and Santa Maria, the US Navy, Brevard County, U.S. Customs and Immigration Service, Shell Oil and Union Pacific.

Errol Ishwara Cowan presently resides in San Diego and can be contacted through ishcow@yahoo.com.

29025076R00122

Made in the USA
Columbia, SC
28 October 2018